The Model's Guide

■ ■ ■

By Rachel Woods

Table of Contents

Prologue

The fashion industry is massive, consisting of designers, stylists, models, photographers, makeup artists, magazines, shops, boutiques and a never ending list of other fashion related jobs. However, this book is entirely focused on one aspect about this industry; the role of the model.

This is a profession that everyone has an opinion on, whether it's positive or negative and whether they even consciously realize it or not.

For example, if the question was asked to you 'what do you think about models?' the general response is unlikely to be 'what is a model?' since everyone has already heard of this profession and they assume they know what a model's life is like. So the responses are usually things like; 'they are rich and famous', 'they are like stick insects', 'they have a glamorous job', 'modelling is great, I want to be a model', 'it's an easy job' or 'models aren't very smart'. This book will hopefully be able to shed some light on what a regular working model actually does and maybe alter a few of those opinions.

Firstly, thank you for picking up this book, since it means that you not only have an opinion, interest or fascination on the modelling profession, but you also want some clarification on what the job is actually like. Perhaps you chose this book because you would like to be a model, perhaps you have a family member or loved one that wants to be a model and you want to understand the job and industry better, or perhaps you are just curious by what you have seen in the media and would like to know more.

However, before sharing my knowledge on the modelling industry, I first need to tell you about myself and reasons for writing this book. I am 5 foot 9 inches tall. This is an average height for a model, however since I reached this height at a very early age and I was always the tallest in my class, I would constantly receive comments that due to my height I should be a model (just for information, not all models are tall, this was just another stereotypical opinion that people had on the industry). Therefore, I was only 10 years old when I had my first modelling experiences by entering competitions that I saw in magazines. I always did well, reached the finals and so I entered more. It was just something fun to do and I enjoyed winning prizes, though because I was so young my education always came first.

When I was 18, my friend from a previous modelling competition entered me into another one (to be the face of a new lady-shave). I won and as a result I was automatically given a contract with a top London agency, so I took a gap year before university and I started modelling full time. I had grown up in the middle of the English countryside and it was a very daunting prospect when I moved to London by myself to work in a job in which I had relatively little experience in.

Like all new models, I had to learn the ropes as I went along. Firstly, I had to learn to navigate my way around a large city in order to find my castings, auditions and work. Secondly, I had to learn what to wear (I was used to wearing jeans and trainers, which I later discovered was unacceptable) and thirdly, I had to learn how to be a model; how to pose, walk, what to say, what to carry with me and how to get good photos.

I had no help. Photographers would just say 'go' and expect me to move around into different poses with no direction, my agency would give me the casting or photo shoot addresses to go to and not tell me what to expect when I got there and since I wanted to look professional to other models (not to mention the fact that they were my competition), I didn't want to ask for their help. So it was only after 6 months and booking very little work that my agency eventually sent me on a 1 hour basic modelling lesson with an ex model. It helped greatly. I discovered ways to correct my runway walk, discovered how to introduce myself at castings and became better prepared for the industry. Of course I still had a lot to learn, but it gave me a little confidence boost. The one thing however that I have never forgotten from my lesson, was when I was told that 'less than 1% of all models make it to supermodel status'. This book therefore focuses on the hard working, average models that form the backbone and other 99% of the industry.

The main aim for this book was to not only give all the information I discovered in my one hour lesson, but everything else that I have had to learn along the way. After nearly a decade working as a model I have been lucky enough to have editorial shoots, television work (including live shows, documentaries and films), commercial, hair and beauty work and have now expanded into TV presenting and of course writing about the industry. However, this book derives from the way that I was initially very unprepared for the industry and I could have benefited from a guide like this. Written to educate all new and potential models and uncover what an average models working life is really like. This book describes the Good, the Bad and the 'Fabulous Darling'!

Introduction

There are often lots of misconceptions about the modelling industry and the life of a model, as our stereotypical image is shaped by 'super-models' and what we are lead to believe by the media. The immediate description that comes to mind is that of glamorous photo shoots, glitzy celebrity parties, fame, fortune and travelling the world. Whilst this is all possible, it is not necessarily an accurate depiction of the life and career of the 'average' model. A successful modelling career depends on several factors; determination, perseverance, luck, timing and skill. Obviously some of these factors such as skill are ones that can be improved and worked on, however other factors such as luck are out of your control. The definition of 'successful' is also one that can be misconstrued. Most people judge 'success' in modelling as having campaigns that everyone has heard of, being photographed on the red carpet, or having a recognisable face in all advertisements. However success can simply be booking a paid job. No matter how big or small, no matter if it gets published or not. To work and earn money in one of the most challenging, competitive and changeable of industries is a success in itself.

If modelling is a career path that you are interested in, it is important to know all the facts about what it is really like and what being a 'model' entails and not base your decision on the pre conceived notion that it will make you rich and famous. *The Model's Guide* therefore aims to give you all the information needed in order for you to make an informed decision on whether it is the right career path for you. It should be thought of as an essential guide to entering the world of modelling as it endeavors to answer all of those usual questions;

"Where do I start?", "how do I get an agency?", "how do I pose?", "how do I build up my portfolio?" or even "do I have the right look to be a model?". Although it not only includes everything you need to answer all of those questions and more, but also displays the pros and cons of modelling in a hopefully insightful and enlightening way and clearly describes the 'real' world of modelling as opposed to the 'media contrived' world of modelling. Throughout this book you will find advice from other professionals in the industry, practice exercises and real anecdotes, which will aim to make your journey into the industry (should you decide you want to model) easier, smoother and hopefully more successful!

Most important things to remember

Firstly and most importantly is to constantly be aware that there is always a lot of competition in modelling. If you are really serious about being a model you need to always put yourself first and make a proactive approach to getting yourself noticed. Model agencies have hundreds of people contacting them daily and as a consequence have no need to search for you. It is therefore essential to make yourself known to them and contact them first.

If you cannot be bothered to make the effort to push yourself, no one else is going to do it for you. Having determination and believing in yourself is the most valuable asset you can have as a new model.

The second most important thing to always keep in mind is the difference between a 'supermodel' and a 'model'. A 'supermodel' can command their own salary for work, up to six figures, they are famous and constantly in the public eye, they dominate magazine covers and designer labels and appear to live the dream lifestyle. A 'model' however is often unrecognised by the public, despite possibly being well known within the industry and they face a hard slog of finding and attending castings, booking work, facing competition and being treated like a human mannequin.

It is only a very tiny percentage of lucky models which make it to 'supermodel' status; the vast majority of models have to work hard at forging a career for themselves, although they can still do well, just without the paparazzi following them.

This book highlights what it is really like to be a model, the parts that the agencies and media often neglect to mention. It is the very rare few models that are in the right place and time to get spotted for a big campaign straight away. It is inevitable that you will get knock-backs, criticism and rejection. However the key to succeeding and ultimately staying in the industry is stay positive and develop a very thick-skin!

1

Overview on modelling

Outline of this chapter:
- Characteristics of what make a model, focusing on; look, personality and knowledge.
- Identifying what sort of model you are.
- Description of the different types of modelling.
- Model measurements

What sort of look should a model have?

There are no specifications to what makes a good model, there are only guidelines. For some types of modelling there are ideal height and measurement restrictions, for other types of modelling there are criteria such as having clear skin, good teeth and shiny hair. Being a model is not about having stunning good looks, some models can actually look very plain in person, but what is essential is looking good on camera and being photogenic. All models however have confidence and should possess an air about them that if they were passed on the street people might look twice, as they should radiate poise or grace, appear to be comfortable in their own skin and ideally have a striking yet natural look. Although the best attribute a model can have is their personality; a model could be the most attractive in the world, but if they have a bad attitude they will not get work. The ideal model look simply depends upon current trends and the look the designer, client or casting director is going for; if a model does not get a job, it is simply because their look did not fit the brief.

What attributes should a model have?

It is a common misconception that modelling is all about the physical look, image or beauty and therefore the personality and emotional aspects are often overlooked. Of course if someone is blessed physically by having good genetics and fast metabolism rate then that makes life easier, however having a good personality is equally important. This means being easy to work with, not complaining, taking the daily competition of modelling in their stride, being very resilient to criticism and above all having the patience of a Saint.

Modelling can be tough; since you are constantly being judged and criticised on the way you look and it takes a strong character to be able to succeed in this high pressured environment. A model needs to have stamina, endurance and have a certain level of fitness, that can enable them to trek around on long days of castings, cope with the pain of holding difficult and uncomfortable poses for long periods of time, wearing high heels, having their hair pulled and tugged, deal with the stress of international travel and handle constant rejection.

As well as having the emotional strength to not only cope with all the rejections and criticisms but also the possibility of dealing with jealousy from people that could resent the 'dream' lifestyle that modelling can offer.

A model also needs to have excellent common sense and be able to adapt to any situation.

Therefore if you think that you have a great look but don't think you could cope with the emotional attributes, then perhaps modelling is not the right career path for you.

Know your stuff!

Okay, so you think you have the look and personality to be a model, but do you have knowledge and common sense? As a model there are two main things you need to know about; yourself and the fashion industry in general.

It seems strange to think that you need to know things about yourself; however you should instantly be able to remember:

- The phone number of your agency (or your own mobile),
- Your measurements (ideally both in UK, European and US sizes)
- Photographers you have worked with. (It is a good idea to write their name and year of shoot on the back of pictures)

Your knowledge of the fashion industry will grow and evolve, however since it is so huge you do not need to know everything about it. Simply an understanding and familiarity about fashion designers, big industry names, latest trends and top models can be extremely useful. It helps to regularly buy magazines, go to clothes shows, wander round the shops or watch fashion TV to keep your knowledge fresh, new and accurate.

You will find that you often have free time, whether it's waiting at a casting or travelling around, so use these opportunities to do something constructive; educate yourself and keep your brain active.

It is also important, if you have a casting and you are not sure exactly who the designer is, look it up online before you go there. As there is nothing more embarrassing than the client asking what you think of their designs, or 'have you seen our website?' and instead of looking like a lemon, with no answer to give them, you can be educated and give them an intelligent answer that will make you stand out.

If you have a shoot do your homework before you get there. Photographer's often have a particular distinct style, so practice any poses that you think might be appropriate.

Always do your research, if you don't understand something, ask! Industry professionals are always willing to help and pass on their own wisdom! You should know your profession. An electrician will know about wires, a carpenter will know about their tools, so as a model it's your job to know about fashion!

What type of model are you?

Next step, to becoming a model is discovering what sort of model you are, could be, or definitely are not. There are many different areas of modelling so you therefore have to realize what sort of model you are and push yourself in that direction. I cannot stress how essential it is that you are honest when determining where in the industry you may fit in. Simply put; if you place yourself in the wrong category, you will not get work.

The categories of modelling can overlap, so there is most likely one, or even several, that will suit you. If you have already tried one category and have faced a lot of rejection then maybe you did not place yourself in the right one. Just because some categories, such as high fashion modelling, stereotypically come to mind as the 'ideal' model type, do not have the misconception that they earn more money, or they can make you more 'famous' than other categories. You can have success in any of the categories.

In order to distinguish which area of modelling you would suit best, you first need to determine what your overall 'look' is. Initially a model is categorised as either having an editorial look or commercial look.

If you have an agency, they will usually determine which 'look' you have. If you do not have an agency, you can determine which look you have based on general characteristics.

Editorial models are classified as having a look that is attractive in a more quirky or unusual way. They have strong bone structures, are slim, tall and stereotypically fit the 'catwalk model' image.

They are often described as being 'edgy' or having striking features. They would usually be seen on the runways or magazines and are more likely to be snapped up by an agency and sent round all the big fashion weeks.

Commercial models are seen as having a look that is more classically beautiful, with softer features and a more 'womanly' shape. They do not necessarily have to be as tall and slim as editorial looking models but need to have height and size in proportion. Commercial models are used for advertising (commercials), beauty shoots, catalogues and would unlikely be seen on the runways.

Commercial models have a look that the public can relate to, hence are used for commercial advertising. Age is not as significant for a commercial looking model, whereas an editorial model might have a shorter career span.

The majority of models can be instantly identified as either editorial or commercial; however there are some that overlap both categories. It is not a problem if you are not easily identified into a specific category, in fact it could even be to your advantage when obtaining work!

The reason this categorisation is important is that it will help your agency (or yourself if you are freelance) with finding castings which are suited accordingly. For example, if a client is organising a photoshoot and specifically asks for girls with soft features, classical 'English rose' look, with slight curves, they are not looking to see strong, edgy features of an editorial model and vice versa.

The same categories would also apply to male models. An editorial male model would have strong features with a chiseled look and a tall, slim physique. Whereas a commercial male model, on average would be more classically 'handsome' with perhaps more shape or muscle.

Questions to ask yourself:

Are you tall (over the height of 5'8"). *If no, more likely commercial*

Do you have 'edgy features' for example, strong cheekbones, big eyes, defined jaw line or unusual haircut? *If yes more likely editorial*

Do you have softer features? Less prominent bone structure, natural haircut, good skin and teeth, long eyelashes? *If yes, more likely commercial*

Do you have a boyish physique, no curves, no bust? *If yes more likely editorial*

Categories of modelling

Now you have decided which type of model you are, editorial or commercial, you now need to determine which category of modelling you would work best in. However, do not be confused by the fact that models have either an editorial or commercial look and there are editorial and commercial categories. A model with a commercial look can still have editorial work; similarly a model with an editorial look can have commercial work.

Also please note that models do not solely stay in one area of modelling, they can overlap. This is purely a guide to the areas of modelling and the one/s that you could work best in.

Editorial (Any work that is printed)
Ideal details:

Either a commercial or editorial model can gain editorial work. However, high fashion magazines, require an editorial model.

Editorial work would include magazines, newspapers, or catalogues, as such any work that is printed and will give the model Tear Sheets (photos torn directly from the magazine) for their portfolio. There are different magazines and catalogues, hence a variety of different types of models are needed. Some magazines just need models to match with a featured article and so can be flexible with look, size and shape, or they might have something very specific in mind. These general editorial jobs are not always well paid, but they can give great exposure and experience.

High Fashion
Ideal Details:
    Editorial look
    Age: 16-24 years old
    Height: 5'9- 6'
    Chest: 32-34 inches, Waist: 23-25 ins, Hips: 33-36 ins
    Dress 6-8 UK, 0-4 US

High fashion models usually have an editorial look and are normally tall with distinct features and can be highly paid. The majority of people wanting to be a model want to be a high fashion model, as these are the ones that are predominantly shown in catwalk shows and high fashion magazines. However, it is also the type of modelling that will have the most competition for jobs. There are different aspects to high fashion modelling;

Catwalk or Runway shows: Models have a strong walk, be typically tall and slender and must display the designer's clothes in an elegant and eye-catching way.

Fashion print or editorial: Some top designers and companies need high fashion models, to represent their brand in high fashion magazines. These editorial campaigns are very well paying jobs and gain the model lots of exposure and recognition.

Catalogue: Normally employ fashion models, but there are exceptions, depending on which brand the catalogue is for. However these jobs showcase the entire range of a designer's collection and consequently it is normally a long shooting day with a vast amount of photos taken.

Commercial
Ideal Details:
    Commercial look
    Age: No ideal age.
    Height: 5'8- 6'
    Chest: 32-36 inches, Waist: 23-27 ins, Hips: 33-38 ins
    Dress size: 8-10 UK, 2-4 US

There are several different categories again within commercial; although they all focus on advertising a product or service and they would use a commercial looking model.

Beauty: Models need to have good hair, skin, teeth and smile. These shoots mostly focus on head and shoulder shots as opposed to full length. Beauty shots are used to advertise things like makeup, cosmetics, or beauty products. Depending on what the shoot is actually for, (magazine, TV, marketing) commercial work can be amongst the highest paying.

Lifestyle: Usually focuses on everyday life, focus is less on the model and more on the company or idea being advertised. There is no particular 'look' that models should have but usually helps to be more attractive.

There are of course areas that can overlap. There is nothing to say that an editorial model won't do a beauty shoot, or that a commercial model can't go on the catwalk. These are guidelines so that you can recognize the differences in modelling, what area would suit you and understand that if you get constantly rejected for certain jobs, then it is probably because it is not the right category of modelling for you.

Glamour

Ideal Details:

Age: 18+

Height, Chest, Waist, Hips all need to be in proportion, although need to have a larger bust size.

Dress 8-12 UK, 2-6 US

This aspect of modelling does not suit everyone, as it implies nudity and a sexual aspect. Models are usually curvier and they need to be very comfortable with their bodies. Whilst there can be nudity in fashion modelling, it is not usually displayed in a sexual way. This type of modelling can pay very well, but you would need to be certain that this would be the career path for you as changing from glamour into fashion or commercial modelling can be difficult, as you could get labelled purely a 'topless model' and could be discriminated against.

Plus

Ideal Details:

    Age: Any (ideally 20's)

    Height: 5'8 +

    Above size 12 UK, 8 US

Not every model is slim. If you are larger with curves, plus size is the best option. However there are still general requirements, such as good skin, hair, teeth, well proportioned bust- waist- hips measurements and preferably taller. Some agencies specialise in plus size models, so it is a case of searching around. A plus size model can feature in editorial work, commercials or advertising.

Petit

Ideal Details:

    Age: Any (ideally 20's)

    Height: under 5'7"

    Dress size: 6-10 UK, 0-4 US

Petit modelling is also an option for girls that are shorter than 5'7, usually slim and who are well proportioned and take care with their appearance (good teeth, hair, skin etc). You can find some model agencies that specialise in Petit modelling, however there are different locations and countries that are better markets for smaller models. It is a case of doing some research and finding the right place for you. Petit models could feature in hair work, beauty shoots, editorials, commercials and advertising.

Part/ feature modelling

Ideal Details:

    Age: any

    Have an ideal body part.

There are options to model a certain part of your body, for example either your hands, feet or legs. This type of modelling can pay very well, however your features must be perfect. If you are modelling a body part, it must be the ideal body part, free of scars, marks, burns and freckles. If modelling hands or feet, nails must be well manicured and looked after, skin moisturised and looking immaculate. It is possible to make a career through parts modelling and you will have to develop a portfolio in exactly the same way as other models, however it can be difficult to get an agent for this type of work, so best thing to do is call around agencies to research if they accept parts models or not. This type of modelling is difficult however, as in order to get the exact shot it might require the model staying still for long periods of time, hence causing cramp, aches and pains.

Many parts models might also choose to insure the body part they model. For example, if a hand model injured their hand they could be insured and covered for loss of earnings, whereas another model, such as a high fashion model would be able to hide any smaller injury and wouldn't necessarily lose any money.

Hair modelling

Ideal Details:

    Age: any (although mostly suits younger models)

    Hair in excellent condition and all natural.

There are many people that just require hair models. Must have attractive facial features as well as, good skin and teeth, however hair is the most important aspect. It must be in excellent condition, preferably long, free of colour, free of extensions and easy to style.

Hair models can be used for exhibitions, hair demonstrations, salon shoots and hair magazines. Although beware of stylists wanting to cut or colour your hair. Only alter it if it would benefit your career and if it is what you really want, don't let anyone force you into changing your look, as you have to be the one confident enough to wear your hair in that style. It is average pay, approximately a couple of hundred pounds for a shoot, however if your hair is being altered in any dramatic way, then it should be a substantial amount greater, upwards of a thousand pounds, as a completely different style also means you have to re-print new comp cards (a models business card) and obtain new and updated portfolio photos.

Kids and Teen
Ideal Details:
Age: under 16

A model can begin their career at any age, from babies to adults however at a younger age it is usually the parent's decision if their child goes into modelling. A child model would still attend castings like any other model, however it is important that the parent takes a back seat and lets their child shine. A pushy or rude parent could potentially affect their child's career in a negative way, as no client would want to book a child model if they thought their parent would be difficult to deal with on set! In order for a child to be a good model they need to be able to take direction on set, be confident in front of the camera and have a pleasant nature. There are no set criteria for how a child model should look, they just need to be cute or quirky; a cheeky smile, braces, teeth missing or dimples can work as long as they have the right personality. However remember that regardless of age, all models face rejection, although it can be particularly difficult for young children to adjust to that. Always ensure that your child is having fun, enjoying modelling and still gaining an education.

Mature/ classic

Ideal Details:

Age: 30+

Height: 5'7- 6'

Dress: 6-10 UK, 2-4 US

A model can potentially work at any age, just because you feel you don't fit into the right age group, does not you should give up. There are many clients that want older models, as that is the look that fits the image of their brand. You would not have a younger model for anti-ageing cream for example. Of course you still need to take care of your appearance, just like any model would and follow the same criteria of having good teeth and smile, clear skin, good hair and maintain a healthy height to weight ratio. You just need to find the right agency for your age group.

Fitness

Ideal Details:

Age: any

Athletic build

These are models with extremely toned and usually muscled bodies. Some Fit models are also professional athletes, so there can also be a lot of competition in this field. There are not usually any other requirements, no height restrictions for example. The only criteria is to have a body that's in really good shape.

Fitness models are used for advertising, editorial or commercial work.

Fitting model

Ideal Details:

Age: 16+

Height, Chest, Waist, Hips: must have exact measurements the designer is looking for.

A fitting model is used by designers to be a human mannequin. They must have the exact height, bust, waist and a hip measurement a designer is looking for in order for their clothes to be tailored correctly for a collection. If the initial patterns or designs in a new collection do not look good or fit well on the model, they will adjust the designs accordingly. Having a fitting model allows the designer to clearly see the garments shape, fit and movement. Depending on who the designer is, pay is by the hour, rather than a daily rate and is normally fairly good, (anywhere from £20- £200 per hour) however it does involve standing completely still for very long periods of time whilst clothes are being pinned and adjusted on the model and numerous outfits will have to be tried on without a break.

It can offer regular, ongoing work, as a designer would prefer to use the same model again.

Alternative
Ideal details: Tattoos, piercings, unusual hair styles.

For individuals that have extensive body art or a clearly individual style, there is a market for alternative models. There are many photographers, magazines or commercials that may require an 'edgier' or 'different' look for their shoot. An alternative model would need to apply for castings in the same way and also build up a portfolio.

Showroom
Ideal Details:
    Age: 16+
    Height, Chest, Waist, Hips: must have ideal measurements for
    the designer

Showroom modelling is very informal and involves the model showcasing the designer's final collection to clients, buyers and customers. There can either be a small runway or the model will stand directly in front of the client. Showroom modelling usually involves lots of waiting around, as a client can turn up to the designers studio at any time of the day and you have to be ready straight away to try on any designs they want to see. In this informal setting it is easy for the designer or client to see the potential in a model and book them for other work. A model can earn good money from showroom modelling as it is usually paid as a day rate and a model would normally be booked for several days at a time. It can also offer regular, ongoing work.

Promotional

Ideal Details:

Age: 18+

Any height or size

Any promotional work involves advertising a client. Models are hired to work at live events, trade shows or exhibitions and the work could involve anything from handing out leaflets, to helping sell items. Whilst there is no set height or size requirements, it is generally the more attractive looking models which are selected as the client would want to attract people to their stall or event. Depending on the particular job, it is not the sort of modelling to gain you much media attention and often it can feel as though this is not a 'proper' modelling assignment; however it can be well paid and is very good for gaining extra income.

Male

Ideal Details:

Age: 16-25 years old (although can work at any age)

Height: 6'- 6'3

Chest: 40-42 Inch, Waist: 32-34 ins,

Don't think all models are female! Men can have equally successful modelling careers although there is just as much competition. They can also be classed as either having an editorial or commercial look and they usually fit into all the same categories as women, although since the age range is often more varied, this can lead to male models having a longer career span. Models must be in good physical shape although do not necessarily need to be heavily muscular; there is also a need for slim, toned models. There are male 'supermodels' although they are unable to command quite the same salary level as some of their female counterparts and they are not as well known to the public.

Details/ Measurements

For any category of modelling you need to know your exact measurements and body details. Do not try to guess what size you are, get a tape measure and find out accurately. It is useful to know your details in both centimeters (cm) and inches (ins) as you never know what a client will ask you for.

Most importantly never lie about your measurements for two reasons. Firstly, don't try and guess what the client wants. You may not be the right size or shape for one job, but you might be the perfect size for another. Secondly, you will be caught out. They will ask you to fit into an item of clothing or take your measurements and it will be embarrassing!

The most important measurements are:
Height: from head to toe (this is the most common thing people lie about, but don't, it will not help you get work!)
Chest: Should be taken around the fullest part of your breast.
Waist: from the smallest part of your stomach, roughly just above your belly button.
Hips: Around the fullest part of your bottom and thighs.

Dress: The clothing size that you would buy if you went shopping. Know both the UK and US sizes

Shoe size: best to find out UK, European and US size

Additional measurements worth knowing:

Inside leg

Bra size (Women)

Glove size (department stores can often measure this)

Hat size (department stores can often measure this)

Collar (Men)

Suit size

Additional details that you can be asked for (although these are easier to remember!):

Eye colour

Hair colour and length

Skin colour

If someone has the attributes to be a model, there is a modelling job out there for them. It is just a case of knowing exactly who you are, being honest with yourself and proactively going after it.

2

How to start getting work as a model

Overview of the chapter:
- How to gain work as a model.
- Explanation of how agencies work and how to get one
- How to find work as a freelance model
- How to start a career through modelling competitions
- Attending castings/ different casting types
- Chapter also includes advice from an industry professionals and author's experience.

From what you have read so far, if you think that modelling is the career path for you, you are probably now thinking how you start getting work? Many people have no idea where to start with a modelling career and so either decide not to pursue it at all, or spend a lot of money on a wasted photo shoot that gets them no-where. So what is the best route to potentially getting work as a model?

Flow chart indicating the different ways to obtain work as a model:

There is no right or wrong way to begin a career in the industry, some people have lucky breaks, others do not, some enter the modelling world quickly and for others it takes time. There are also several different avenues that can be taken in order for an individual to start gaining work as a model. As indicated above the main route is to find an agency, who will find you work. However, there are other options such as working as a freelance model, whereby you place yourself in the shoes of an agent to find your own work. Or you can try entering a modelling competition; if it is sponsored by a reputable agency it is a good place for being spotted. As an alternative there are other options such as modelling schools or conventions (large fares for models and industry professionals to meet), although these are not the best routes to go down (hence they are marked with a dotted line on the flow chart) as they are expensive, generally not needed and are unlikely to help at all with a modelling career. The main thing is to have a clear goal that you want to achieve and remember that only you can decide whether or not you want to model and try the different routes to accomplishing this aim.

Agency route

The agency route is the best one to try initially as a new model. Once you get more experience the freelance route becomes easier, however an agency can help set you on the right footing for the industry.

How does an agency work?

A concept to think about is that an agent or agency should work for you. To help you find work, negotiate your fee, solve any problems and generally act as a 'middle man' between yourself and the client. In turn, you should therefore consider yourself as an ambassador for the agent rather than an employee; you are the face that the clients will meet and you need to represent your agent in a respectful and appropriate way.

The more commonly known choice of representation is by a model agency and depending on size they might allocate you to a personal 'booker' (agent) or all the bookers might collaborate together in finding you work. Or you could be represented by a singular agent, which is not as large a business as an agency, but can offer a more personal one on one approach.

However, finding someone to represent you can sometimes be a daunting task for new models as there is a strong fear of rejection. You might get lucky and join the first agency you contact, or it might take several attempts. Just remember not to take it personally if they say 'no', it simply means you do not have the right look for them at present and you should try another one.

It is very easy to get discouraged when you hear rejection from agencies, but you need to keep thinking positive and believe that any agency that says 'no' to you, that it's their loss and they missed the opportunity of working you.

Please be aware though that whilst it is useful to have an agency and it does take a certain amount of perseverance to get one. If you have bravely soldiered on and tried every agency you can find in your area, more than a few times each and you are still not having any luck there are a few things to consider; You might want to try a different type of modelling, perhaps you placed yourself in the wrong category and are finding the wrong agencies for your look. Perhaps you are not contacting agencies in the way in which they want to be contacted, or you are not sending the best or most appropriate photos of yourself to them. You could go freelance, as you don't necessarily need an agency in order to get work, or you might not be entirely suited to being a model, so could change career path slightly and train to be the makeup artist, or photographer. As remember the model role may seem the more glamorous option, but the crew behind the scenes can still get paid equally as well, still get to travel and still meet the same celebrities that models can!

Having an agency can make your life easier than going free-lance, as they contact the clients, arrange the castings, confirm the payments and try to get you work, so your main job is to turn up and be amazing! However, there is one aspect that agents don't always make known (or it may simply be an unconscious thing) is the fact that they often have 'favourite' models. The handful of 'elite' models are deemed by the agency as being particularly special and more unique than the hundreds of other models on their books and are consequently nurtured more, pushed forward more, supported more and are therefore more likely to reach the 'super-model' status.

It is often a catch 22 situation, in the sense that if a model is 'in demand' (meaning highly sought after for work) they will become a 'favourite' model amongst the agency and be pushed forward more. However, it is only after being pushed forward by the agency in the first place, because they felt there was potential with the model, that they became 'in demand'.

Nonetheless, for any model to be taken on agency books, they obviously would have thought in the first place that they have a good look, image and are 'model' material.

Most agencies might claim that a model able to make it to 'supermodel' status might be discovered once in a blue moon and it is essentially the Holy Grail for any agency. However, it could also be argued that the 'supermodel' look is very subjective and the status has mostly been achieved due to the forcefulness of the agency in pushing them forward, which as a consequence they become more in demand and therefore with the right backing from the agency and with the same level of attention any 'average' model on their books could potentially reach stardom.

How to get an agency

There are different routes that you can taken in order to become represented by agency:

- An agency scout can find you.
- Entering modelling competitions or attending events.
- Contacting them directly: by post, email, or in person.

1-Scouts

Many top agencies will send out scouts from their agency in order to find potential models. A scout can spot you anywhere; at the supermarket, airport, nightclub, or walking down the street. If a scout discovers you, it is purely down to luck and you just happened to be in the right place at the right time.

If you want to increase your chances of potentially being spotted, there are usual places where a scout is likely to be, for example, at a large event like the 'Clothes Show' or around top fashion spots in big cities, such as around Oxford Street in London. If a scout stops you, it is because you they are interested in your look, as you have the right look for their agency. They will give you their business card with their contact details in order for you to make an appointment to come into the agency to meet with the other book-ers and to potentially be taken on their books. If you get scouted there is no guarantee that you will be represented by that agency, however the chance of them saying no is reduced. Under no cir-cumstances would a model scout ask you to part with any money or ask for your personal details and make sure you fully check the credentials of the agency on their business card before organising any further meetings with them.

2- Attending competitions and events

There are many fashion events, competitions and pageants that can help you to find an agency. It is an accumulation of you pushing your-self forward for the event or competition and in return the agency approaching you and showing an interest in wanting to represent you. Even if you don't win the competition, you can still spark the interest of an agent, as they would be looking for someone with potential.

3-Contacting agencies directly

The best way to contact agencies directly is to have a look on the internet for lists of reputable model agencies. In the UK, the AMA (association of model agents) posts a list of all registered agencies. Also check your local area and do some research on the internet in order to find a recognised agency. Once you have found a list of reputable agencies, look on their websites and gage from the type of models they represent which agencies would be best suited for you.

Submitting your photos to an agent

Check agency websites to find out the preferred way of contacting them.

Some agencies have electronic forms on their website for you to submit your photos and details immediately, some prefer email, or the good old fashioned postal method and others have drop in times for you stop by the agency in person.

What to send
Via Mail:

Send them a brief covering letter, 2 or 3 photos and self stamped address envelope.

You want to keep the letter as brief as possible, as the agencies are not interested in your past modelling experience, interests, reason for modelling, or anything else you may feel the need to write down. All they want to see are your measurements, contact details and photos.

An example of the letter can read:

Dear Sir/Madam.

I am interested in joining [name of agency].
Here are my details:
Height:
Chest:
Waist:
Hips:
Shoe:
Dress:
Hair type:
Eye Colour:

I have included some photos for your consideration.
Look forward to hearing from you.

[Your name]
Contact details. Email/ mobile/ website etc.

When sending the photos, do not inundate them with loads of shots. Two or three pictures can be enough. Do not panic if you are new to modelling and are worrying that you have no professional photos to send them. They actually accept and prefer amateur shots taken on your own camera.

When models have professional shoots, the pictures are edited, re-touched and altered to make you look good, however by sending amateur photos without all this fuss, they can see the real you.

Whilst snapshots are acceptable to send, this does not mean that you can send photographs taken with someone else and say that you're 'the one on the left', or pictures of you on holiday holding a giant cocktail in your hand. They want you and only you in the photo and they want simple shots.

Take pictures in front of a plain background, ideally a white wall. The essential photos to include are a close up shot (head and shoulders) looking straight to camera with no smile (like a passport photo) and a full length shot (head to toe), however it is also useful to include a side profile. They want to see you with no or minimal makeup. Hair can be down one photo and tied back in another. Ideally have no jewellery or piercings in the photos and look as natural as possible. Wear something simple and tight fitting, so your body shape is clearly shown (skirt, shorts and tank top is acceptable).

Make sure that you write your contact details on the back of your photos as well, so if they lose your covering letter and just find your pictures, then they can still get hold of you.

Finally the stamped address envelope is so they can send your photos back if they are not interested. As there is no sense spending extra money repeatedly getting photos printed off when you can re-use them and keep trying again! Or they can send a letter of response back to you.

It is better to contact as many model agencies as possible. Send at least 10 envelopes initially to 10 different agencies. If they are interested in you, they will usually contact you to schedule an appointment to meet you in person. This does not necessarily mean that they will take you on their books, but if you go there confident, friendly, smiley, natural and dressed appropriately, they will have a hard job turning you down!

Via Email

Same method as via postal mail; you can use the same letter template and add the same photos as attachments (making sure that the photos are attached as Jpeg or Pdf template, in order for their computers to open the files without problems).

It is best to send one email at a time, so you do not let all the agencies know that you are just applying to everyone, you want to make the email personal and address it to each individually, so they know you are interested in them specifically, rather than just desperate to find an agent!

Open call times

An alternative way to contact agencies is to attend their open call time. Most agencies have a set time and date in the week for new models to stop by in person. You will need to check the individual agency website to find out when their open call time is.

Attend the open call in the same way as if you were called for an interview with them; prepared with photos and looking presentable. However, you might face a waiting time, as guaranteed there will be several other models waiting at the same time as you. If you are able to travel there, the main advantage of attending an open call is that the agency can see you are serious about your career, want to do well and that you were confident enough to show up unannounced, as well as the fact that you usually have an answer straight away if they will take you on or not, it is just a quicker way than waiting for the postal system to deliver your mail and then wait for a response. However the main disadvantage is that it can sometimes be very daunting walking into the agency, as some do not have a reception area to be greeted straight away, you can end up walking straight into their office and if you are new to modelling it can be upsetting having a rejection face to face. However it is the probably the most recommended way of finding an agency and it allows you to see what the agency is like, meet the bookers if you are successfully taken on, or get constructive feedback if you are unsuccessful.

Meeting the agency

All agencies work in slightly different ways so there is no set way on how to behave or what it will be like when you first meet them. However as a general guideline:

- No chewing gum,
- No chaperones, friends, parents, etc (unless under 18years old)
- No head scarves, hats, headbands, sunglasses, or any oversized accessories that are going to distract from your face.
- No oversized clothing, no maxi dresses, large hoodies, baggy T-shirts etc. They want to see your shape; safe clothing option is skinny jeans, heels and tight fitted top.

Usually if they have invited you in, they will want to have a chat with you and ask you about yourself: What sort of modelling you are interested in, what age you are, what location you are based in, if you are willing to move locations, have you signed with any other agencies, have you had any experience, etc. they just want to get an idea of what you're like. It is not always just looks that they are after; they want to know what your personality is like, as you are representing their company.

They will probably ask you to bring in more photos with you. If you have professional ones, now is the time to show your portfolio, however if you are just starting out, they will happily see more amateur shots. They will normally want to take their own photos when you are there (the same type of shots that you initially submitted, but they will usually take the pictures on Polaroid camera), to see if you are confident in front of the camera and how photogenic you are.

If you are under 18 they will ask you to bring a parent or guardian with you, however make sure that you do the talking. They want to hear from you, as you will be the one speaking at castings, so they need to make sure you are confident enough to speak up yourself. That does not mean that the person accompanying you has to sit there in complete silence like a statue, it just means that you have to take charge of the conversation and don't let anyone else answer questions or talk for you. Use your own voice!

Agencies will usually tell you there and then whether they want to take you on, it can sometimes be a very quick decision, or sometimes the bookers at the agency will discuss you for a while.

If it is a 'no', keep smiling, ask for any feedback to improve your chances next time and most importantly, thank them for their time, as you never know if they will change their mind and contact you in the future. If it is a 'yes', be pleased, obviously thank them, but don't go crazy, they want to know that you are still professional. Carefully check over any contract given to you and clarify any details about the agency and how they work before definitely committing yourself to anything (it is ok to ask to take a contract home to look over; you do not have to make any decision immediately).

Contracts

If they want you to join their agency they will present you with a contract to sign. Make sure you take it home, read it carefully and fully understand what you are signing. They are normally standard contracts, but if you any questions don't be afraid to ask your agency or have it checked over by a lawyer. You do not have to limit yourself to one agency; just make sure you read the small print to find out exactly what the terms of your contract are and understand exactly what you are signing. Contracts can either be exclusive (meaning you can only join that one agency. The only way you could join another is with their permission) or non- exclusive (meaning you are not tied to that agency, you can join others, but check the small print to see if you would still have to give them commission from work gained from the other agencies). The standard agency commission is usually 20%.

Once you have official signed with an agency: how to they work?

Divisions

When you walk into an agency the first thing you will usually spot is the vast amount of mini slots on the walls which display a model picture and a handful of their cards. These photo walls are known as the boards.

Depending on the size of the agency they will usually have different boards and divisions. When you first join the agency you will be placed on the 'New Faces' board, which is self explanatory, as you are either a new face in the industry, with limited experience or a new face for that agency. There is no set amount of time for how long you remain on this board, it just depends how much experience you gain and how quickly. If you are still in education, you might remain on this board longer and generally men move from it quicker than women.

When you become more established, you will then be moved up a division to on the 'Main Board', which is then divided into a main board for men and a main board for women. This is the largest board as the majority of models will end up on it. Depending on the size of the agency there will also be extra divisions for plus or petit models, parts models or models that have travelled from abroad and they do not look after them as the mother agency.

Once you have found an agency, signed with them and they have put you on one the division boards, it is important to build up a good rapport of working with them; get to know the bookers and think if them as an extended family. Your agent is neither your employee nor your boss, you should be on equal level and co-operate together. Although, you need to remember, that since you are not an employee of the company you are not entitled to usual employee benefits, such as healthcare, sick pay, or holiday pay. You work with your agency, but as a self employed model. Your agency is there for support, if you have any problems or questions you should feel comfortable enough to talk to them, so always have an open line of communication with them.

Since you can be assigned one booker or several, it is useful to find out who you will be working mostly with and find out how many other models are also assigned to them, so you can gage how much attention you will be receiving.

They will have lots of models on their books, so it is important for you to keep in contact frequently with them in order for you to be remembered.

Some agencies have offices that you can drop into and others you will have to keep in contact with via email or phone. It is advisable to stay fresh in the booker's memories as they may have a job to fill last minute and if you have recently contacted them, they will be more likely to think of you straight away and book you in for the job.

There can be long periods of time when you hear very little from your agency and might not get many castings and the ones you do get are general ones where you know there are going to be hundreds of other girls and you are not that likely to book the work. It is therefore easy to become really frustrated with your agency and you might feel that they are not looking after you as best as they could be. This occasional lack of castings can either be attributed to a genuine quiet period in the industry, where there really isn't much going on at all, or it could simply be the truth that they aren't looking after you and are more focused on their top more 'in demand' models, so the other 'average' models can sometimes lack attention. There are also times, such as fashion week, where the editorial models are given more attention, as they are booking more work and the commercial models are a bit forgotten about. This is a little bit understandable as when the show season is on, it is going to be the editorial models that will be booked for the shows and therefore earn the agency more money at those times.

It is always useful to find out from your agency what sort of model you are, whether they think you are more editorial or commercial and the sort of work that they might therefore put you forward too.

Some agencies will particularly push some models for certain jobs, however for the rest of their models they are likely just to send them in bulk to general castings, in the hope that they might be lucky.

Therefore, if you feel that your agency are sending you for the wrong sort of castings, ones that you have little chance of getting as you are not the right look that the client is after, you must speak to them. Find out if there are other castings that you can go to that are more suited to the type of model that you are.

Booking out/ availability

First of all, before you get sent to any castings or work, the main thing that you should be aware of as a model is that your booker will always assume you are free unless you tell them otherwise.

'Booking out' is the term used when you inform your agency of your availability, or specific days that you cannot work. A client can book you for any day, including the weekend and your agent will always assume you are available unless you specifically let them know. You must 'book out' the times or days you are not available for, as there is no use afterwards once you have been booked to do a shoot, saying that you are actually not free that day. Always update your agency of availability and any other details that it is important to tell them.

Mother agencies

Depending on conditions of your contract, there could be no limits to how many agencies you are allowed to have. Most models, however, have a 'Mother' agency that is essentially their main agent and the one that they would initially go to for support. Their mother agent would then ideally look for other agencies around the world to collaborate with and send their models to. Most models need to travel internationally in order to expand their career and gain more exposure and experience. So a model could have their 'mother' agency in one country and have several other subsidiary agencies in other places. However, once the model has travelled to the subsidiary agency, it is up to that agency to find them work and look after the model, it would not be the responsibility of the mother agency to find the model work for that period that they are away. There is no set amount of time for how long a model will travel for, it could be anything from a few weeks to a year, it often depends on the amount of work being received, how comfortable the model feels being away, or personal choice of the model. Always check all conditions of a contract as commission can be paid to more than one agency; you may be entitled to pay 20% to your mother agency plus 20% to the subsidiary agency, hence you then lose 40% total of your pay instead of the usual 20%.

Copy books

Some agencies hold a copy book or spare book for you, which is identical to your portfolio. This is normally used to send out to clients or other agencies around the world. For example, if your mother agency is in London, they might send your copy book over to another country, maybe Japan, France, Italy, or Greece, to try and find you an agent over there, so you can gain some international experience. It can also be sent to clients to get you more castings or work, or it could simply be used in case you ever forget yours (which you should never happen anyway!) A model can have several copy or replica books. Just remember it is usually at the expense of the model, if their copy book is sent via courier to other agency. Therefore, if you do have a copy book, ask your agency to let you know when and where they are sending it in advance, to avoid too much surprise additional expense.

Additional costs

Reputable model agencies will of course not take any money from you up front; however there may still be additional charges that you might not be expecting. Such as, the above mentioned courier fee for sending your copy book out. If you travel abroad, your agency will probably say that they will cover the cost of transport or accommodation, however, you will have to pay them back from future earnings and if you don't get enough work then you will be in debt to the agency. They might order new comp cards for you, without checking with you first and then you will end up paying for them. Or some agencies ask you to pay a minimal fee for being on their website. Therefore always ask your agency if you are likely to incur costs and always check your earnings statements from them carefully.

Authors Experience

I had a good relationship with my first model agency; I got on well with all the bookers, had frequent work and was perfectly happy with staying them. However, after I had spent a year and a half working with them and modelling full time, I decided to take a slight break and attend university. During my university break, I decided to go back to my agency for a visit and see if they had any work for me whilst I didn't have any studying to do. I was extremely surprised to find that they had moved office without telling me! On tracking them down, they were apologetic, really friendly and still had me represented on their books, so I didn't mind too much. However, this  should have been a warning sign, as on my second visit a few months later, they had closed the agency down and disappeared! I finished my studying, got my degree and carried on modelling on a freelance basis; it was only by chance a year later that my agency re-emerged under another name, although I did not work with them again. I later found a new agency however this was a strong lesson learned that you should never rely completely on your agency, still look out for your own work and never let anything bring you down or stop you achieving your dream.

Advice from an Agency/ Booker

Cynthia Saldana (founder of Ikon New York
Model Management)

There are so many models with the right look to work in this business, so having a great attitude and personality is everything.

Amanda Rushforth (Model and agency booker in Dubai)
From a model view: soak your face in moisturizer the night before a shoot, bath in milk and apply cranberry juice on the hair! From a booker view: Polaroid's are important and to make sure the images you book models from are airbrush free! Always turn up and on time! The best advice I could give is never be late. I wish you could push the ones that do more, than the ones that let you down... but it's always the one who is most in demand that will let you down.

Freelance route

There is no need to put your dream and your career on hold if you are unable to find an agency, as there is always the opportunity to go freelance.

As a freelance model, it means that you find your own work without an agency, promote yourself and since you would not be contracted to anyone, you are able to decide who you work for and when. Many models go down the freelance route, as there are many people in the industry that look for models, but are reluctant to pay the agency fee and so advertise jobs directly. You can still find freelance work even if you are represented by an agency or agent, but check the details in your contract with them, as you may still be liable to pay them their 20% percentage, even if they didn't find you the work, so essentially you could be giving them money for doing nothing.

How to find work as a freelance model?

Admittedly there are a few jobs whereby you might need an agency to promote you and you would be unlikely to get yourself as a freelance model. Such as booking the major catwalk shows for the main fashion weeks or big advertising campaigns. However, on saying that, there was an occasion where a well known cosmetic brand placed a casting call online for a major TV commercial and the casting did not get sent to any agencies. This is a very rare occurrence although it is possible it could happen again.

It can be a slow start to freelance modelling, as you have to build up your own contacts and find your own work. However with time, you will notice that you will be asked to do work, instead of always finding it yourself. As the same people want to work with you again or your name gets recommended to others.

In order to initially build up these contacts, you need to search for work and promote yourself as much as possible.

There are numerous websites that you can join (most of them for free) that connect models, photographers, stylists, makeup artists and designers. Sites such as:

www.modelmayhem.com (free)
www.istudio.com (free)
www.starnow.co.uk (minimal cost- subscribe for 3 months to a year)
www.onemodelplace.com (free)
www.modelmuse.com (free)

There are many other sites; these are just examples of popular ones. These sites contain many casting calls, offering both paid and unpaid work, which you can apply for, however as a freelance model you need to be very motivated and you have to frequently check the casting calls online every day, as one day missed could mean opportunities lost.

Of course you must be aware that on these modelling websites that anyone can place an advert, so a small minority may not be legitimate. It just takes some common sense to decipher which jobs are worth applying to. If you are unsure about working with someone, look at the examples of their work or their online portfolio, ask them for references and speak with someone who has worked with them before.

In order to apply for these jobs online you need to sign up to the individual websites and create your own profile page.

What to include on your profile page

Firstly, you will need to start your profile by writing a paragraph on yourself (and remember to check your spelling). This is a snapshot for anyone viewing your page of the type of model you are, your level of experience and your personal characteristics. General example can be as follows:

Hi, thanks for viewing my profile. I am from *(location where you are from/ currently working)* and I have been modelling for *(amount of time)*. I have experience with/ I am looking for *(beauty, hair work, runway, glamour, lingerie, commercial etc)* assignments. I am *(very reliable, punctual, friendly, confident, open to shoot ideas, experienced, willing to learn, sociable etc)* and I look forward to working with you soon!

For the next section you will be asked to submit your statistics. Something that I cannot stress enough in this book is not to lie about your measurements or details. If you are booked for a shoot based on incorrect measurements, the photographer or client will not be happy and you will probably be asked to leave the shoot. On the other hand you could also be missing out on opportunities with photographers and clients that actually need models with your exact size. Don't try to guess what the client is looking for, just be yourself.

Finally, add your photos. It is extremely important that your page on these sites is professional and you only showcase your best photos on there. If you are brand new to modelling and you do not have any photos to add on to the page, then ask a friend or family member to take some of you. These should be simple ones, exactly the same as the ones you would use to apply to an agent. Take close up head shots (looking straight ahead, turned slightly away and side profile), minimal to no makeup, some with hair tied back, some with hair natural and some full length shots (make sure these are taken from waist height since it can make you look out of proportion if pictures are taken looking up or down at you).

With some sites you are limited with the amount of photos you are allowed to add onto your profile, therefore if you already have professional modelling photos, make sure that they only display your best work. To aid you with choosing your best photos, my profile is displayed on Starnow.com as a good example of a models portfolio. This should help you decide which pictures showcase your different looks and demonstrate how versatile you can be.

Maintaining your profiles
It is very important to maintain all the modelling and media sites that you are on. This means updating your photos regularly and ensuring that your statistics are always accurate.

Do not set up your profiles and then sit back and wait for people to contact you; you need to make a proactive approach to getting work and building up your contacts and friends list. You should therefore be checking all your profiles on the different websites and the casting calls on a daily basis and responding to any messages you receive as soon as possible; ideally within 24 hours. Even if you are not interested in working with someone, it is only polite that you respond and tell them that. As well as the usual standard messaging, there are also other ways people can contact you, such as adding comments on your photos, writing TAGS (general comments on your profile) or adding you to LISTS (lists of photos that they have found that they are interested in) or friend requests. If you receive any comments like these, it is polite (and good for making contacts) if you send a message in response, just saying 'thanks for your message/ comment/ tag/ list it would be good to work with you sometime'.

You can join these sites at any stage in your career, from amateur to professional, although they are particularly good for new models as they offer a way of building the contacts up and developing portfolios.

Contacts
This industry relies upon the catchphrase 'who you know, rather than what you know', indicating that you could be the most fantastic model in the world, but without the contacts, no one will ever find that out. You should think of your collection of industry contacts like a house of cards. In the sense that they can be difficult or time consuming to build up, but once they are established they will stay in place. They can also come tumbling down just as quickly if you do not look after them; either by not keeping in touch or not being professional.

How to make contacts (as a freelance model)
You will start to build up your database of contacts fairly quickly if you are smart, professional and friendly. Simply the more experience you

have and the more work or castings you attend, the more industry contacts you obtain.

The main thing is to always make the effort to talk to people, or if they speak to you first, make sure you communicate in return, even if you are not a naturally chatty person. This does not just apply for castings or shoots, but also whenever you are out and about walking, on public transport or anywhere where you are in a situation where you can chat to people; as you never know when you will run into that one contact that could make your career. Never assume anything about a person's appearance. You may think that someone dressed more casual may be an assistant at a shoot, but could in fact turn out to be the director.

It may also go without saying and apologies for stating the obvious, but always be friendly to everyone and even if you have any negative thoughts about someone, keep them to yourself, as you never know where that person may end up in the future. If you are rude to another model for example, you don't know if one day that model could end up being the client, or casting director and you may have lost the opportunity for more work.

Whoever you speak to in the industry, it is advisable to get their business cards. Try to obtain as many as possible and keep them in a safe place. When on a shoot, get business cards from the MUA, photographer, stylist, or anyone else you are working with at the time. Try to send them a thank you message after the shoot, as it shows you are professional and they are more likely to use you again or recommend you to others. Similarly, always carry a comp card with you, as your portfolio can sometimes be heavy to carry, so you might not have it with you at some shoots, but at least you still have a card in your bag. If they have your card, it is an easy way for them to contact you again.

Network

There are many modelling social networking sites that aim to connect industry professionals. Used wisely they can build up good contacts.

You can find people to shoot or test with, find good examples of other modelling work and find out about castings. However make sure you set up a professional webpage yourself, which best showcases your work, in order to get people's attention. Just remember that if you ever receive a message, whether you are interested in the work or not, always reply promptly, a late response can mean work lost.

Some social networking sites, however, could hinder your career. Whilst they are a good way of keeping in touch with people in the industry you have worked with, sometimes they can also see all of your personal life. It can therefore be a good idea to have separate sites. (one personal, one professional) as sometimes friends can post embarrassing pictures, or write funny comments, some of which may not be very encouraging to a potential employer or client. Therefore if you want to be friends with a photographer or MUA, etc, it is better to invite them to be your friend on a more professional page, where you can add your portfolio and it looks more like you are a serious model, rather than a party animal with your friends!

Events/ Parties

In order to network, you should also aim to attend as many events as possible that you are invited to. If you receive any invite where there will be other industry professionals attending, you should always try and go, as events are a great way of building up more contacts in a relaxed, sociable setting.

Just remember, don't over-do the partying too much, models still need to have a decent amount of sleep, as they need to stay looking refreshed for work the next day!

Who is the right person to know?

The essential idea is that the more contacts you have the more work you can bring in. Although there is no specific person that you must know in order to succeed in the industry. It could be a case of finding the right agent, meeting a designer or photographer or having someone in your family that can push you forward for work. The latter option is always frustrating for most working models, as some people get a boost in the industry from having a parent or close family member that is already a celebrity or well –known personality. There are some models that are the offspring of rock stars or actors and they only get modelling work and often prestigious high paying work, because of their famous connections, but possibly wouldn't otherwise have had the opportunity to become such a top model. For all the other models that are striving to build up their own contacts, in can seem like an unfair advantage for celebrities to have their own family pushed forward just because they are famous.

Average working models have to compete for modelling jobs not only with other models, the children of celebrities but also the celebrities themselves. Many actors, singers and TV personalities are featured on magazine covers, campaigns and advertising and are taking over what is essentially the model's job. Therefore the more contacts you can build up and the more you can push yourself in the industry the better it will be for you; the only way to overcome this frustration is to get the work.

Competition and Pageant route

The experience gained through actual modelling competitions or pageants can be a good place to start. They will not only give a good basis for learning to deal with the competitive nature of the industry, but especially for new or freelance models, they can offer a step in the right direction to becoming a professional model.

There are a vast majority of pageants and some are better known than others. They usually involve raising sponsorship money for a charity or for an entrance fee into the competition, however they can offer a good start into modelling as they are normally organized by a model agency (check whether your competition has a known and reputable agency behind it) and they usually provide good media coverage.

The best way to find out about modelling competitions or pageants is to regularly check your local newspaper, check on modelling agencies websites, regularly scan magazine covers or search the internet.

Modelling competitions and pageants can be a good start for getting used to the industry, as they give valuable practice of walking the runway or striking poses for having pictures taken. Although there are a couple of differences that you would need to remember if you transcend from the pageant world to the high fashion world.

Pageants require a particular stance when posing. Usually feet in a ballet position, with feet at 45 degree angle to each other and one hand on hip. This is a generally accepted pose. However on a high fashion runway, it requires a bit more simplicity and a less of a stylized position.

Smiling is also an obligation in pageants or competitions, you will probably have to smile until your face hurts, however in modelling a more serious, thoughtful or expressive face is needed.

If you are fortunate enough to win the competition or pageant, a modelling contract with the organizing agency is usually offered and the more competitions you enter the more chance of you getting noticed. It is a good way to get your foot in the door and a fun way of meeting more contacts.

Note to remember with the pageant/ competition route is that whilst competitions are a good place to start and gain experience, remember that they are exactly that a 'competition', you are there not only to get exposure in the industry, but to compete and to win!

There are of course always speculations and rumours at some pageants that they are a 'fix' and they already have winners lined up. This is true for some of them, but you still have to maintain the mindset that you have just as much chance of winning as anyone else. Make a real effort, always have nails, hair and makeup looking perfect, wear something eye catching, take your time on the runway and don't rush your pose at the end of it. Make frequent eye contact with judges, smile constantly, get involved with the competition as much as possible and always place yourself in positions where you can easily be seen.

There is always a massive amount of competition with other models, but you cannot let yourself be fazed by this, you have to make yourself stand out and having the practice of competing in pageants can sometimes be advantageous. Even if you don't win the competition, the agency involved in the still might want to take you on their books anyway.

Whatever route you take into the modelling industry, the main thing is to remain focused and keep pushing yourself. There are always ways into the industry if you have all the right attributes to be a model. If you have tried all the possible ways you can think of; freelance, agency route, competitions or alternative routes and have faced constant rejection, then unfortunately it is probably best to find another career choice with the industry.

Casting types

Finding an agency or promoting yourself down the freelance route is unfortunately not enough; the hard part comes when you start to attend castings. Some jobs can be booked directly (hence known as a direct booking) without a prior meeting with the clients, however the majority of the time you will have to previously attend the casting (like a mini job interview) in order to get the actual work.

If you are a freelance model you are limited with the castings you will get, however if you are an agency represented model you are likely to get a variety of casting types and probably more of them.

The two main types of castings are those for photographic work (printed, editorial, magazines) and those for commercial work (TV, adverts, campaigns).

As a rule of thumb always get prepared before walking into the building. Do not get caught by surprise. Do not walk in with your hair a mess, change your footwear if need be before walking in, take your coat off, get your portfolio out your bag and do anything else you need to. It could be the case that you will go straight into the casting, or you could have a long wait. Either way, you don't know who will be there at the other side of the door when you walk in, so make sure you have a good entrance.

For photographic castings:
On arrival they will usually take a Polaroid picture of you. The person taking it will not care if you get a good photo or not, so you have to quickly prepare yourself as best you can.

Tips: stand straight in front of the camera. If it is for hair work, bring your hair forward over your shoulders, if it is for teeth work you should smile, think about what the casting is for. Then turn to the side (they may say show profile). Tuck your hair behind your ear so they can see your face. Stand straight, look directly forward and keep your mouth closed and eyes open.

When you are called to the casting director(s), firstly shake their hand strongly and immediately hand over your book.

Directors will often flick through books very quickly (which can seem a bit off-putting at first like they are either not interested in you or just being rude. Try to resist the urge to say anything to them, they are taking note of your work!), sometimes make comments, take a comp card (which should be in your book) and hand your book back. You can then thank them and leave.

For commercial castings:
These are often filmed and you may receive a script on the day. Importantly try not to panic, as you will tense up and not look as good or relaxed on camera.

The most important thing, even if you can't remember all the script, is to know the name of the product (and pronounce it correctly!)

For many castings, although mostly commercial ones, they will ask you 'what's your name and where are you from?' The most common mistake for all new models (and sometimes established ones) is to say where you live or the place you're from, when they actually mean 'what *agency* are you from?'

Follow any instructions and then give a card, thank them and leave.

Photographic and Commercial castings can then be broken down into different casting types:

General casting:

This is the main way of seeing a client, also known as a 'cattle call' due to the large volume of models that attend whether they are suitable for the job or not. Castings are open to all agencies and all models (unless the client is looking for something specific, blond hair and blue eyes for example and then the casting would not be open to brunettes or red hair models) and they are usually held between a designated time frame so the models do not all turn up at once. Castings are normally very busy and a lot of models can attend, there are normally sign in sheets, so make sure that you write your name down as soon as you arrive, or if there is no sheet, find out which model was the last to arrive, so you know your position in line. Do not feel intimidated by the large number of other models there, remember to stay focused on yourself and stay confident.

In the US however your booker will have to electronically submit you for some castings and then if the client likes you, you will then attend the casting. So it can be difficult to actually get in front of clients, let alone get the job.

Some general castings can be frustrating, as you might wait a long period of time before it gets to your turn to see the casting director or client and then you might spend less than a minute in front of them. For some particularly busy castings they will flick through the models portfolio very quickly, take a comp card and instantly decide there and then if the comp card will go on the 'yes' or 'no' pile. It can be very disheartening if you notice your comp card being assigned to the 'no' pile (which can be easily identified as the larger one!) and you might actually feel like asking for your card back again, (as they are about £1-1.50 per card and you don't want to waste them) but try to resist that urge! However at least you can gage straight away if you have that job or not, it can actually be more discouraging if you feel that you have just had a really good casting and you end up having a very promising vibe that you will be successful in booking the job and then you discover that you have not been chosen (just for clarification you will never be contacted to inform you when you have been unsuccessful in booking a job and you will not get any feedback). In these situations try to keep your chin up, stay positive for the next casting and you never know if that client will come back to you in the future, or want to book you for another job. Some clients will end up keeping your comp cards and might contact when you least expect it.

General castings however are a good way of making more model friends, as you are very likely to run into the same models again at different castings. If there are models from your agency going to the same castings as you, it can be nice to travel around together to all of them, so that you have some company.

Go-See:

This type of casting may not be for any job in particular. It is usually where the agency will contact their clients and say they have a great new model that they recommend the client sees. Therefore when the client does need a model, they will have already met them, seen their book and have their comp card with contact details.

The client may have a job already in mind, but it is normally a general meet and greet and a good way to build up contacts.

Requests:

Most sought after casting, as request castings are normally for bigger modelling jobs. The client would usually be the one to contact the agency and request to see a certain model. However in some cases the agency might have particularly pushed the client to see their models. You would normally have a specific time in which to turn up and it is essential that you make that time slot.

Call backs:

If a casting has a large amount of models apply, or if it is for a particularly well paying job, the client might want to narrow the amount of models down and compile a shortlist of them to see again. This second casting is a 'call back'. It is seen as a very promising sign to get a call back, as it displays the level of interest from the client and there is more chance of booking the job.

It would be unlikely to have more than one call back, but of course for big campaigns or advertising where they need to ensure they have the right model, the client might arrange a several call backs.

Keep Calm

Castings can sometimes be very tedious and stressful, however as a model you need to be very adaptable, keep calm and do your best. There are no set amounts of castings you can receive; you could have one or several. With regards to time and distance, they can either be very close together or far apart. Casting times can also change last minute and you might be sent away and told to come back later, or the agency can accidentally send you to the wrong address. You have to battle through crowds of people, or slow public transport. You need to attend castings whatever the weather, it could be pouring rain or scorching heat and it can be very frustrating having a long journey to get to your only go-see casting of the day only to be seen for a couple of seconds, for no job in particular, just for a meet and greet. Just put everything down to experience and try to think that when you get a booking it will make all of the hard work and effort at castings worth it.

Summary

In order to get started in the industry, you first need to try different avenues to being noticed, hopefully get an agency, attend castings and then that will lead to work coming in. Do not expect this to be a quick process. Even if you have an agency, it can take a few months of attending castings to book your first job, or if you are going free-lance it also takes a long time to build up the contacts. You need to have patience, perseverance and persistence!

3

Working on a Shoot

Outline of chapter:
- Details on booking a job
- What to expect when attending a photo shoot
- Working with photographers
- Working with Makeup Artists
- Working with Stylists
- Working with other models
- Authors experience
- Advice from industry professionals

Once you have received and accepted an offer of work, you will then attend the 'booking'; meaning you are booked for the job and you are therefore unable to accept any other work that conflicts that day. If the booking is for photographic work, it will be referred to simply as a 'shoot'. Or if it for runway or catwalk it will be referred to as a 'show'. All other work can just be called a 'booking'.

Booking details

Your work should start the day before a shoot; making sure you are completely ready, know where you are going, have everything packed in your bag and have done some research on the internet on the client or photographer who you will be working with. As this can give you an idea on their style and roughly what you can expect when working with them.

Whether you have booked a job from an agency or as a freelance model, you should receive a 'call sheet', giving you all the details on the job and what to expect. If you don't receive a call sheet, make sure you ask for all the booking details! Ensure that you fully understand the job and double check all the details beforehand. Such as:

- What exactly is the job for?
- If it is a photo shoot, what is the potential usage of the pictures?
- What is the payment?
- Where is the location?
- Who is it working with? (Plus get contact details for the photographer or someone else on set, in case you have any problems getting there or finding them).
- Times and how long will you be needed for?
- Will you need to bring anything with you?

It can be very exciting when you have booked a job, there is the sense of accomplishment and obviously it is very pleasing to know there will be money coming in. Although there can be the unfortunate occasion where a shoot can be cancelled last minute, or you could actually arrive at the location and then be told that you are no longer needed, thereby losing out on payment and losing money for travel expenses. This is not a frequent incident, as it is very unprofessional. If this rare occasion ever occurs it is either due to the model being late or simply the client changing their mind.

On Arrival

Firstly arrive early or on time, never late. If the booking is for a shoot, ensure you gain an understanding beforehand with the photographer and makeup artist about what you all expect from the outcome of the shoot; what look you are trying to achieve, what is the 'concept' of the shoot and what ideas do you want to try out. This shared vision will allow the shoot to flow more easily, you will have fun and the pictures should turn out great. If you do not understand the concept of the shoot, then communicate with the photographer or makeup artist, they would rather clarify the ideas for you, rather than have you be confused or tense up on camera.

One aspect when on a shoot that can seem very bizarre at first to a new model, is that there is no sense of personal space. The model is essentially the blank canvas that is being used to create the perfect shot, therefore in order to achieve the perfect look and turn the canvas into a work of art, it is completely acceptable to touch or alter the styling as needed. You can fully expect to have your outfit adjusted whilst you are holding a pose, have your hair constantly re-arranged, makeup touched up and other alterations frequently made that you might not notice yourself, but the photographer will spot straight away through the camera lens.

(Makeup touch up during shooting)
Photo by Lisa Michelle Photography

Where are photo shoots?

A shoot can be held anywhere. Generally they are either referred to as being set in a 'studio' or on 'location'. A studio is set indoors, in a purpose built room with professional lighting, backdrops and props. There are also many photographers that have set up professional studios in their homes, since it saves the cost of hiring a studio and they already have all their equipment there.

If a shoot is on location it simply means 'out of the studio' and therefore will either be shot outdoors, or in a location that would not normally contain a studio set up; for example a hotel, museum, or gallery. If the shoot is on location, ask where the base will be setup, so you know where you will have your makeup applied or a place to change.

How long will a booking last?

The length of time for a booking depends completely on what the job is. A show, for example, would involve a clothes fitting a few days beforehand, arriving a few hours early on the day of the show for hair and makeup, then the show itself could be 15 minutes. A trade show booking could last all day from 9am – 6pm, or even a few days. A fitting job, could be anywhere from a couple of hours to all day. Photo shoots also have no set time period, it just all depends on what the shoot is for. However, they can be very time consuming since it sometimes takes up to a few hours to have makeup applied, another hour or so for hair and styling and another couple of hours for the photos to be taken, as there could be many outfit changes or different locations.

Different roles on a shoot

A shoot can either be just the model and photographer working together, where the model would be expected to do own hair and makeup and bring a selection of clothes. Or it can involve a whole team of people, all working together to create an agreed concept.

Model: That's you! You are the subject that is expected to give life to the photo and portray the concept of the shoot through your poses and expressions.

Photographer: The one that will take the images set up the lighting and find the best location to shoot in. The photographer will also spend hours after the shoot reviewing all the images and editing the best photos.

Makeup Artist (MUA): Makes the models skin look flawless and design the makeup appropriately to suit the style and theme of the shoot.

Hair Stylist: Simply to style the models hair, to match the theme of the look with the MUA and fashion stylist. However a hair stylist is not always present, for some shoots the MUA will also be responsible for hair (whether they are a trained hairdresser or not).

Fashion Stylist: Not always present on shoots, if they are attending they are responsible for supplying the clothes, dressing the model and working closely with the MUA to follow the same theme of the shoot. If there is no stylist, the model may be asked to bring a selection of clothes.

Assistants: Again not always present, but they can assist anyone on the photo shoot to provide an additional support.

Working with Photographers

The photographer is the one that is going to get you the amazing pictures you want for your book, as they not only set up the perfect lighting, location and take the pictures, but you also need to remember that their job is not completed at the end of a shoot like a models is. Some models do not appreciate the amount of work that can go into one shot, as they may only have spent a day working and then receive the final image. The photographer actually has to spend more time, not only arranging the shoot, but they actually keep working on the photos, for hours, days or even weeks afterwards, searching through hundreds or thousands of shots taken to find the best ones, then editing and altering to make the pictures look the best they possibly can.

Here is an example below of a strip of pictures (which are all extremely similar) that the photographer would have to look through and determine which is the best in order to select for further editing and become the final image.

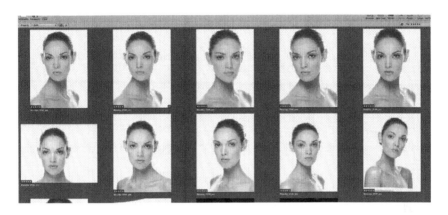

(Computer screen shot displaying the selection of images)

(Final edited version that would be given to the model)
Photo by Stefan Wegmüller

In understanding exactly how much work a photographer will do, it will aid the collaboration with them. You also want to work well with the photographer, since they are the one that will give you the pictures and hopefully book you for work again.

Working well with the photographer means you need to co-operate and communicate with them. You should be ready to shoot when they are, follow their instructions, listen carefully and give great poses. However, it does not mean that you should do something that makes you uncomfortable, for example, if they ask you to suddenly do a nude 'body' shot and you are not happy with that or made aware of it before the shoot, then understandably you can politely say no and not do it, but in general take the direction from them, as they want the good shots just as much as you.

Sometimes a photographer may give you lots of direction, which is really helpful and especially great if you are a new model, however, sometimes they may just say 'go' and leave you to pose completely unaided. This is called a 'rolling shoot', where you need to think quickly and move effortlessly and fluidly into different poses. That is why you need to know how your body works, practice poses in the mirror beforehand, be confident enough in front of the camera and know what you are doing. So that if you get given no direction, you will not stand there like a rabbit caught in headlights!

The Set/ lighting/ photography

The photographer has the job of arranging the set (the area where you will be shooting). They will set up the picture with adequate lighting and background and whilst you do not need to know about photography and lighting techniques, it can be useful to familiarise yourself with some basic knowledge. For example, if they are using a slow shutter speed on the camera, you need to hold your pose completely still for longer, otherwise it will blur. Most photographers tend to use digital now, but if they do use film, ensure that you are in the best possible position to get the shot. With digital you can try different poses and play around a bit with movement, however with a limited number of pictures on each film, you have to be on form for every shot. With regards to lighting, if shooting outdoors, you could suggest a location where you think the natural sunlight would be best, or if you are in a studio, think about where the photographer has set up the spotlights and angle or position yourself to efficiently catch the light on you.

Without doubt, it can feel very strange on set to have so much equipment around you, however you just need to focus on what you're doing, yet still be aware of what is surrounding you and listen to the photographers.

Set surrounding model   Finished photo from the shoot
Photos by Lisa Michelle Photography

Model Release Forms

Some photographers might ask you to sign a model release form at the start or end of a shoot. They are more common when you are working as a freelance model however they are fairly standard procedure with some photo shoots. By signing a release form, you are giving the photographer permission to use your image and photographs. It allows them to edit, alter, crop or photo-shop the pictures and to use them in any way from personal to advertising. However, these forms are nothing to be worried about, the photographer will not use the pictures in any inappropriate way, as they want good photos as well and they want to make a good reputation for themselves, just as much as you want to have a good reputation. Admittedly it does not protect or benefit you as a model in any way, it is solely designed for the benefit of the photographer; to protect them from any form of liability and allow them to sell the photos in the future for commercial use or advertising and not need any further permission from the model.

You always need to read the release, although photographers will always give a copy of the photos to you and allow you to show them, either in your book or online portfolio. Note: when displaying your photos online, always credit the photographer's name. This is not only good etiquette but generally a stipulation of the release you would have signed. Signing a release will still allow you to show your pictures although not sell them on to any advertising yourself.

Therefore release forms are generally fine to sign, provided you have read it thoroughly and completely understand what you are signing.

Working with MUA (Makeup Artists)

Depending on budget constraints and the type of shoot, some makeup artists will also act as the hair stylist. Firstly when turning up at a shoot always have clean hair and face. This means no hair product on and absolutely no makeup (you may hate to leave the house like this, but it has to be done). If you have short hair it can be easier to manage, however if you have long hair, ideally wash your hair the night before the shoot, as it will make it easier to style. If you wash your hair that morning your hair will be silky smooth and more difficult to control.

It sounds disgusting, but dirty hair is better to style than clean hair (just do not have your hair too dirty or greasy, remember you are still a model after all).

Many people enjoy having their makeup applied as it feels like being a celebrity for a day; having someone else to pamper you and make you look glamorous. However, for models, having makeup applied is part of the job and it can often be quite tedious. It can be very difficult sitting still for long periods of time, or it can feel uncomfortable or unpleasant having makeup constantly applied, removed and re-applied, especially around sensitive areas like the eyes. Whatever the case may be, feel free to talk to your makeup artist, let them know if you are feeling uncomfortable, don't think you have to suffer in silence because it's your job to be the model. If you like the look they give you, tell them, they want their art work on you to look good, just like you want your art work in front of the camera to look good. However, unfortunately if you do not like the look, then there is nothing you can do about it. It would be considered completely inappropriate to alter it, as your job is to display their work, you don't have to like it. You could suggest changes if you really thought your makeup didn't look right, but do not alter it yourself.

You will also find that the more frequently you have your makeup done, the more you will get used to it. It will gradually become less uncomfortable, you will adapt to sitting still for ages and you will learn how to move your facial features to aid the MUA. Such as, when having eye makeup applied, you need to look in different directions; eye liner applied on the bottom left side of the eye lid, you need to look up to top right, always look the opposite direction to where the MUA is working, or tricks such as pursing your lips in the correct way to make it easier for lipstick to be applied.

One major factor with makeup is hygiene. Makeup artists could work with more than one model on a shoot, or they could have just come from another busy job, so you need to ensure that the brushes and equipment they are using are clean. The vast majority of makeup artists are extremely considerate and hygiene is part of any makeup artistry course, however there can be the rare few that either don't care or don't think about your health as a model. While you don't want to seem like you are complaining, you have to look after your face and skin. There are many unpleasant things that can be passed on through unclean hands, brushes or lipsticks for example and you cannot afford to get spots, cold sores, rashes or anything else from an unclean makeup artist, as it could not only affect your chances of getting the next job, but more importantly affect your health.

A few little things to look out for:

- Make sure the makeup artist has washed their hands before starting work on your face (or used gel hand sanitizer).
- Use a clean sponge/ brush to apply foundation
- Use a disposable mascara wand
- Use a brush to apply lipstick (they do not apply the stick directly on your lips)
- If anything important falls on the floor make sure it is washed thoroughly before being used on your face again!
- If any false product is applied to your face, such as false eye-lashes, or stick-on-diamonds, make sure that they are all easy to remove before they are applied. Check with the makeup artist what glue is being used.

It's mostly common sense; however speak to your makeup artist if you have any concerns, allergies or questions. Your face is an extremely important part of your job and your main selling point, so look after it!

One fun aspect however is the fact that after you have completed the shoot, you can either choose to remove your makeup, or keep it on (no matter how outrageous) and see how many looks you get on your way home. The latter option has the best entertainment value!

Doing it yourself!

You will meet many different makeup artists who will all have their individual style, so it is always a nice idea to pick up advice from the makeup artists you meet. Ask them what their one top tip would be, as this will help you if you ever have to do your own makeup for a shoot. It could be a clever way to put your eyeliner on, such as burning it slightly with a lighter to make it soft, or it could be mixing different lip glosses, using a certain sponge or brush to apply the foundation, or simply using moisturiser. You don't always have to use the tops tips or listen to the advice, you might think some of them are great and some you wouldn't try. But whatever it is, it is always useful to know what works for your skin and how to bring out the best in your look and you never know when that top tip could come in handy!

Working with Stylists

Many people incorrectly assume that because you model all of these fabulous clothes, you get to keep them. This is unfortunately untrue. There might be occasions whereby you are allowed to keep an item or instead of being paid in cash you might be paid in clothes, (which is great if you really like the clothes that you will be paid with). Although on the other hand, you don't get to choose your outfits and even if you don't like what you are wearing, you have no choice but to accept it. If you know there is going to be a stylist at the shoot, it is always a good idea to let them know your exact measurements in advance so that they can supply the wardrobe in your size. It means that they will already have the clothes and the style of the shoot planned out, however it is always useful to have a pair of black high heels with you, as shoes can sometimes be the one thing that can cause problems and a selection of underwear, as you don't know what the outfits will be like.

If there is a stylist, remember that their role on the shoot is to assist you with wardrobe changes which may include adjusting the clothes whilst they are on you, or actually helping you into delicate or tricky outfits. You need to be comfortable working with the stylist, however remember that you are the model, you are essentially a mannequin to them and they are not interested in the slightest at seeing you semi-naked, all they care about is making the clothes and styling look good.

However, again, feel free to speak to your stylist and let them know if you feel good, uncomfortable or want to try more looks.

It also may seem like common sense, but do not ruin the clothes. Be careful not to smudge your makeup on any garments when getting changed, do not eat, drink or smoke when wearing the clothes and if there are any tags on items, do not pull them off, as they may be on there for a reason.

Working with other models

There will come a time in your career where you will have to work with another model, or several other models. Do not think of them as competition, but rather as an additional friend to work with.

The most important thing is to concentrate on what you are doing, do your best and do not be put off, intimidated or distracted by the other model(s). Just be yourself, don't try to copy them, as it will not look natural, pose in ways that are comfortable and suit your body. If you try to duplicate someone else, you will lose your unique style that the photographer hired you for in the first place. Also, since you will likely be working in close proximity to each other in the same shot, it is advisable to have a mint for your breath and body spray, as it makes things more pleasant!

Time

A photo shoot usually goes quite slowly and is often very time consuming, however when there are several models at a time, then it goes even slower. You have to expect to have long delays and wait your turn to be called. Do not jump ahead of the queue of models to get your makeup applied quicker or photos done faster, as the chances are you have to stay until the end of the shoot anyway

Working together

It can feel disappointing if you think that another model has a better outfit than you, or superior styling, but unfortunately you do not get a say and you just have to cope with it. The choice of outfits depends on the individual model and what the client feels would look better, it is not a case of favouritism.

When sharing the same frame (photograph) it can feel like you are competing with the other model for the best position, but do not try to take over the picture, you have to share the space. If you start to get frustrated or annoyed it will show in your face and will not come across well on camera. Just remember you are still in the photo, still getting paid and it's your job. So if the photographer tells you to stand at the back of the picture, suck it up, go to the back and be amazing, chances are if you act professional and come across as a good team player they will want to work with you again.

You have to work well with others, as you may have to pose closely together in a photo, so being positive and friendly will make the shoot easier and more enjoyable. If for whatever reason you don't feel comfortable with the other model you are with, have a private word with the photographer, do not announce it loudly how unhappy you are.

The vast majority of the times, shoots with other models are a good laugh and you can have a lot more energy in a photo and meet some new friends in the process, as guaranteed you will run into the other model(s) again, probably at the next casting!

Have fun!

Above all, a photoshoot is meant to be an enjoyable experience and collaboration for everyone involved. It is a great chance for everyone to make new friends and contacts. Essentially, the more you communicate with each other and the more fun you all have on a shoot, the better the photos will look, for everyone!

Authors Experience

In my many years modelling I have been fortunate enough to have some great experiences, although like all other models, there are some experiences that are best forgotten about!

One of my first modelling jobs, for a major hair product brand, involved having my hair cut live on stage, followed with a catwalk show afterwards. I was informed by my hair stylist that it would be nothing drastic, just a slight trim, however once I was seated on stage in front of 200 hairdressers I noticed large chunks of hair falling to the floor. Since there was nothing I could do, I had to remain seated until he had finished. The end result was a nightmare, my once beautifully long hair had been cut short on one side, had sections randomly chopped out of it and was an odd asymmetrical style. He not only ruined my hair (until it managed to eventually grow out) but he was also extremely rude and insulting. Since this was one of my first jobs, I thought everyone in the industry was rude like this and it nearly put me off modelling completely. Thankfully my hair grows quickly so I didn't have to put up with the dreadful style too long and I was given loads of free hair products and a decent hair cut as an apology and luckily I kept modelling and didn't let one bad experience ruin not only my hair but my career.

Like most women I like to keep my eyebrows nicely shaped, so when a MUA offered to do them for me, I thought that would be fine. What I made the crucial mistake with is that they plucked them without a mirror in front of me. I commented several times that it felt like they were taking too much off one than the other, but they assured me that I was looking fine. Unfortunately for me, I did not stop them when I started feeling apprehensive and I ended up having nearly a complete eyebrow removed! So if you feel unsure about anything, go with your gut and do not let anyone alter your appearance unless you are convinced they know what they are doing.

When I had a shoot for a national newspaper modelling a beautiful Asian Sari, I felt really elegant wearing such a decorative outfit. However, due to all the little decorations; small mirrors and beads attached to the Sari, I found that I was unable to move for fear of crushing all the adornments, not to mention the heavy weight of the outfit. Since I had to remain standing completely still for such a long period of time, I started to feel a little faint. I warned the photographer that I wasn't feeling too good, but he kept insisting that he was nearly finished and to hang on a bit longer. I did however end up collapsing, fell off the raised stage, into a heap in front of the photographer and crushed the dress that I was trying so hard to avoid damaging! Once I had recovered I carried on shooting and the crew around me were luckily very helpful, however if you ever feel unwell make sure you tell the crew and take a break.

Advice from the professionals

It can give a little extra confidence on a shoot, to know what a photographer, MUA or stylist expects of you as the model, so here are a few bits of advice from the experts themselves.

From the photographer

Lisa Weatherwax- Arhontidis

I would say the best attribute a model can have is to be kind and friendly. Sounds basic but I love being able to connect with a model, to laugh, be silly and just get along! Makes the end result so much better and I know I'll have a lasting friendship with them and will want to work them again!

David G Fisher

If the model is waiting, talking or laughing with the crew on set, they need to have the ability to almost instantly move right into poses with confidence when the photographer is ready to take a shot. So, I'd advise a new model to look through magazines like Vogue, or the online portfolios of famous models and study the poses the models use in the most impressive photographs. Memorize and practice them in front of a mirror until you can transition from one to another smoothly and confidently. Continually add new poses so you have plenty to draw from in any situation, whether the shot is a close-up, full body, sitting, etc. If you can do this and also take direction well, then you will make the photographer's job much easier and you'll quickly earn a reputation as a talented model.

Michael Hallenbeck

My practical advice for those wanting to enter the modelling industry...

The modelling industry is tough and there are many people looking to get ahead and step up to the plate. It takes a lot of commitment if you want to make it a real career. If you have the look and are someone that is adaptable in style and looks, first off start test shooting with as many professional photographers as possible in your area. Make sure they are legitimate and have online available work and references.

If you set a shoot date with a photographer, commit to it. The night before the shoot, don't stay out all night, showing up with red eyes looking like a mess and don't cancel last minute, unless it's an emergency.

Assess the best direction your particular look will take you, what your goal is and go for it.

It's essential to have good chemistry or vibe with the model. Both the photographer and the model have to be open and explore creatively together. Listen to the photographer's directions, though if you have reservations with what will be expected of you on a specific shoot, you must discuss it with the photographer or your agency first, so there's no misconception on the shoot.

I always tell my models to "live in the space" and open up, don't hold back, get a bit wild inside and that expressiveness will come through in the work.

"Mental homework" is my other word of the day. I ask my models to do mental homework while giving them a specific direction. I direct the shoot as it's an acting exercise and when I say "Give me pensive", I want you to be doing whatever you need to do in your head to have that expression come through and be genuine.

Sometimes I also have my models let loose and do a little freestyle dance for a minute...it helps loosen up the uptight ones, trust me! Just let go, live the moment, be in the moment and make excellent art.

Dipesh Lakhani
We all make mistakes when it comes to our craft, but that is how we grow and develop into better Models, Photographers, or MUA's.

The most important thing for me in terms of working with a model is adaptability and open-mindedness, especially when trying something outside of their comfort zone. These two ingredients foster a great creative environment.

Also, with creative directors, photographers and clients trying to find common ground in terms of vision and direction of a shoot can be difficult, so it's always refreshing to work with a model that is easy to get along with and nice. Just be yourself!

I had the opportunity once to work with an amazing creative director, who has worked on many photo and film shoots over the past 25 years lending a creative hand to make ideas come alive. When we were scouting Models she was confident that as long as we had models that were willing to follow instructions and feel the emotion that was trying to be evoked we could get the photos we were after. She was exactly right!

Jeff Bevis

I am a firm believer of safety first! So, if a model doesn't know the pho-tographer. She can bring an escort (a girl friend or a guy friend) never a boyfriend. Why not a boyfriend, because if the boyfriend is nearby or in the studio, the model will be distracted. If a model has to go to meet a photographer by herself she should carry some sort of spray (pepper spray) for protection. Another thing I talk to new models about is posing. I tell them to check out other models and study their posing on the internet, magazines and so on and practice the posing in front of the mirror. The more a model knows their craft the more valuable she or he becomes.

Stefan Wegmüller

Some things I would tell an aspiring model would be:

Firstly, befriend an older, established model to whom she could have as a mentor.

Secondly, keep a folder of 10-20 "must know" poses and PRACTICE them until they become 2nd nature; the model should be able to strike those aforementioned poses in a state of "being" as opposed to "trying".

Thirdly, find a way to *really* like the photographer they'll be working with, even if they have to fake it. Nothing will kill an entire shoot quicker than if the model has even the slightest hint of distaste for the photographer, especially for an up-close beauty/head shot session.

Remember that everyone loves a "pleasant" attitude and more importantly the camera doesn't lie and picks up every minutia of detail.

Also be impeccable with messaging. Respond to agents, photographers or bookers the SAME day, never more than 24 hours after message. Effective communication is key and be very specific with questions and answers.

And finally, be 100% reliable. Although to a newcomer the industry may seem huge, it's not. There are only a few big name houses, photographers, agents etc ....nothing will destroy a career quicker than developing a reputation of being an unreliable or difficult model to collaborate with.

Stephanie Apple

I've found that one of the quickest and easiest ways to shoot with a model is to talk with them before the shoot and of course during the shoot. It makes the model more comfortable and makes for a better vibe on set. Also you need to have fun and establishing the verbal relationship is part of that. If no one talked and we (the model and the photographer) just did our jobs it would be a very boring shoot and it will show in the photos.

There are two main reasons you shoot, either for yourself (building a portfolio, for fun, for your client, etc.) or for the model (to build their portfolio, for their fun, for their client, etc.). Going into the shoot with a well thought out plan will allow you to utilize time and be efficient, but it will also allow the natural flow to go much better.

Pay attention to details. Notice things that may be out of place, such as rings or earrings that don't match the outfits, or necklaces that shouldn't be in the shot, chipped nail polish, hair fallen out of place or one shirt sleeve longer than the other.

When directing a shoot, if I ask the model to twist, turn and tilt their head, shoulders or body, rotate clockwise or counter clockwise, it should be small, controlled movements most of the time.

Give compliments to each other; it boosts moral for everyone on set when everyone is in a good mood and the end result will benefit.

From the Makeup Artist (MUA)

Anni Bruno (photo: Stefan Wegmüller)

The number one piece of advice I can give to a model hoping to gain favour with their makeup artist is to show up with a clean face. If the model shows up to the photo shoot with her makeup already done, that's a BIG no-no and a sure-fire way to tell the makeup artist that you don't trust them to do great work!

Also models probably don't realise it, but in order to get every tiny bit perfect on the makeup design, they are required to look up, look down, look to the side, etc. So, if they are texting or chatting, that makes the makeup artist's job a lot harder. Best thing to do is really focus on getting 'prettified' and listen to the artist's instructions. It'll also make the makeup chair time go a lot faster.

Always turn up to the shoot on time and be courteous and friendly to everyone on the set, even if you're not sure what their job is. Work hard, thank everyone when the day is done and if you particularly liked the photographer/makeup artist/hairstylist, refer them in the future and they will do the same!

MUA's don't mind having to do touch-ups, but when a beautiful, perfect, dramatic lip shape has been created, try not to mess it up by eating, drinking or smoking. Try to do these things before application and the MUA will thank you for it!

Finally, MUA's appreciate having to do less work, because time is always of the essence. So the model can cut down a lot of time by showing up with good skin. This can be achieved by having proper rest and hydration (drinking lots of water), avoiding diuretics like alcohol and caffeine and getting regular facials if you're prone to breakouts. The more work you do to keep yourself looking fresh and rested, the less work the makeup artist will have to do, the day will go faster and everyone will thank you!

Deborah Fulton - Mellor

Firstly, be aware that you are normally one of the last people to be involved in the shoot. The Photographer, Stylist, Makeup Artist and other members of the creative team would have spent a lot of time working out the looks and themes for the shoot, so don't expect to walk in and have any control over the look. Modelling isn't about looking pretty; it's about communicating the look and vision of the creative team. So whether you like the makeup or not, work with it, it's shows you have the mark of a professional.

Be flexible. People will always remember flexible, professional people. I'm always asked to recommend good models and the ones that sat fiddling with their phone, pulling away when I'm trying to apply eyeliner and huffing and puffing rarely get their name passed on.

Soak up everything you can from the people you work with. Remember that everyone from the Makeup Artist to the assistants will have worked lots of shoots before and are a bank of knowledge. So don't be afraid to ask them questions. Makeup Artists end up being the 'mum' of most shoots anyway, calming nerves, drying up tears, even supplying tampons! They'll normally be willing to help! Lastly, do your research. Don't expect to turn up and 'wing it'. If the photographer tells you the influences are 'Galliano AW08' mixed with 'film noir', then research them. They'll tell you it because they want a specific look and they need you to deliver it as quickly as possible. Studio space is very expensive and they want to get as much done as they can in the time booked. Also take a few minutes to check out the photographer's website; do they have a specific style? It would be good to practice any recurring themes you notice, they will appreciate that.

Darvell Freeman (Photo: Stefanie Apple)

For all the years in the industry working with models my advice is to be a professional and bring your best performance to each job. Be prepared and on time to shoots, with clean face and hair and nails manicured and pedicured. Have several undergarment pieces handy with a good pair of pumps in your bag. Carry a small makeup bag with your basics essentials: a perfect foundation, concealer, mascara and lip balm with colour and blush. Know the fashions and trends of the season, designer's names and have a passion for clothes so you can understand what you're wearing and become the vision. When working with a team of artists always remember it takes everybody to make it happen, so always shine and let the light follow.

Ha Sun Shim

I guess every job requires punctuality, but it is especially important for the models, as if they have not arrived on set, then no one can start work! It happens quite frequently and in my working experience it can definitely ruin their reputation, because in that field of work it is all about making a good impression, networking and there are many other models waiting to take their place.

Another thing, that is important to mention; whilst the makeup artist is putting on the makeup to your face or any other part of your body, do not be distracting them with crazy boyfriend texting! It is okay to use your phone if it is urgent, for an agency call or if your work schedule changes, but don't bring your personal love life to the work area. Makeup artists are 'artists' who put colours to canvas, but if someone is distracting us in the middle of the painting, the result may not be as good as expected.

From the Stylist/ designer

Helen Rhiannon

A few bits of advice I would give from a designer's perspective:

For castings, wear well fitted, simple clothing so you show your frame and body shape well. No baggy clothing or clothes which are distracting.

On a shoot, take a selection of underwear as you may need to change the colour or fit depending on what you will be wearing.

Don't be shy! The worst thing for a designer is when someone is shy when changing...they only want to see the clothes and really aren't bothered about seeing anything else!

Listen to the team and don't question what they are saying as you are just the clothes horse and you are working to a brief for them. Remember that you are trying to recreate their vision. If they ask you to do certain poses, try your best to work well with them, but if it's uncomfortable, tell them and take short breaks so you don't get cramp. It's not as glamorous as people make out sometimes but the end results are worth it!

Annabel Tollman

Best advice for a new model is to be 200 percent professional. Know who you are working with; what's the magazine, who is the client, photographer, stylist? Do your research, know your references. Be enthusiastic and give your all to the shoot.

That's what makes a great model; being one of the team and being interested.

4

Being Prepared

Overview on the chapter:
- Building up a modelling portfolio
- Details on composite cards
- How to stay organised
- Essential items to carry in your bag
- Punctuality
- Author's experience

Since all models (agency represented or not) are self employed, it is essential to be well prepared in order to give the best chance of getting work and continuing to book future work. This means being organised, punctual and having a well looked after portfolio. If a model lacks these basic attributes it will make working in the industry even harder.

Business material

The main items that a model needs to be prepared with at all times are their portfolio (book with photos) and comp cards (a models business card). These are essential for any model, regardless of whether they are a new model or very experienced.

A model's portfolio/ book

Every model in the world should have a portfolio (otherwise referred to as your 'book'). It is a book that is completely individual and unique for each model and displays a collection of the best examples of the models work. It is comprised of a selection of different photos, all showcasing the models range of styles, expressions and versatility.

Most importantly, do not expect clients to view your photos on a memory stick, disc or any other storage device and do not have snaps printed out, you need to have a proper book. Since a portfolio is the most essential item for any model, to attend a casting call without it would be likened a Doctor attending to a patient without their medical kit.

A 'good' portfolio is subjective; you are never going to please all clients all the time. Everyone is going to have their own opinion on which photos they like and which they don't, the only thing you can do as a model is make sure that you display a wide variety of different looks and expressions, as well as a range of movement and poses.

A models portfolio should never really be completed, as they take time to develop and with experience the pictures in it should be changed and updated constantly. As a models personal look changes, with age, or a new hairstyle, their portfolio must update with them. A client wants to see what the model looks like now, not how they looked a couple of years ago.

You need to be unbiased when selecting what photos of yours look good and which ones should be included in your portfolio. It is important to find a balance when viewing your own work, as it is easy to become either very biased, thinking all your photos look amazing or be too critical, by thinking they all look really bad. Try to imagine you are viewing a stranger's pictures, think what lighting is most flattering, what angle or pose is better, what the overall photo looks like; is it interesting, boring, eye-catching, vibrant or dull? You always need to be impartial when analysing your photos, not only for placing the right ones in your book, but also as a learning exercise for getting good pictures at future shoots.

Take care

Your portfolio should be treated with respect, which includes keeping the pages clean, not adding extra scraps of paper in the back, not using it as an umbrella and not damaging or scratching the cover; it should always look presentable when showing it to a client.

Also take care of it at all times and try not to lose it! As models are rushing around all the time, at castings or shoots, it is easy to forget about your book and leave it on a bus, train or taxi. If this ever happens, ensure that you have copies of all of your photos. If you have tear sheets, make sure you buy the magazine twice to have a spare copy, or take photocopies of pictures. Try to have an electronic copy of photos saved and have either your agency or your direct contact details inside your book, so that a Good Samaritan might return it to you.

Building a portfolio to approach agencies

With so many photographers willing to do tests with models (they get a model for free, the model gets pictures for free; win-win situation), there is no need for a model to spend their money on developing a portfolio. Do not feel that you have to have a portfolio before approaching model agencies. This is a common misconception, which leads aspiring models to spend a fortune on photo shoots to get pictures that they can put into a book to show agencies, when in fact it is completely unnecessary. Any good agency will help you build your portfolio and find you good photographers to work with for free. In general an agency would want to develop your book in their way and style. In order to do this they have may have photographers they prefer their models to work with. Most importantly do not feel embarrassed if you have just started modelling and your book looks very sparse of pictures. Any client will see what you look like in person and will not judge you if you don't have many shots, they know that everyone has to start their career somewhere and as long as the couple of shots are good ones, that is all that matters. It is all about quality over quantity.

Types of pictures

Tests

Any agency taking you on will help you start your portfolio by arranging 'test shoots' for you, or as a freelance model, you can contact photographers directly and ask for a test.

A test shoot is an unpaid shoot and is exactly that; a 'test'. The photos are usually for portfolio use and they are normally for testing something new for the photographer, such as a new lighting technique, or new camera. Or for the model, such as testing what look suits them best, trying out new ideas, or adding variety to a portfolio. The idea is that the photographer will get to work with a model for free and in return the model will get pictures for their book.

The majority of portfolios are initially made up of test shoots. Even established models occasionally take test shoots, as it is a good way of refreshing your book and building more contacts in the industry.

Some photographers may contact you and offer you Test for Prints (TFP), meaning exactly that. A normal unpaid 'test' shoot in return for the photographs. It is advisable to use your own judgment whether you accept the work or not. If you have seen the photographer's portfolio, you like the type of pictures they shoot, you have checked references, you know the shoot is only for personal portfolio use or if your agency recommended you work with them, then by all means go ahead and shoot with them.

However if the photographer or client says that the shoot is for a magazine, look book or any other form of advertising, where your image will essentially be gaining profit for them and they don't pay anything, then it can be seen as unjustified and unfair to ask you to work for free, as clearly they will be earning money from the publicity, but you will not.

They might entice you to work with them by saying you will get 'tear sheets' or excellent exposure, which might well be true, but at the end of the day this is not going to pay the bills.

You wouldn't hire a plumber or carpenter for example and not pay them for their work, so why would you not pay a model for their work? If it is a genuine 'test' shoot then as a model and especially a new model, you should not really be turning them down, however if the work is being portrayed as a 'test' yet someone is actually benefiting financially from your advertising or editorial work, then you are entitled to get paid. Modelling is a job like any other job and you cannot earn a living from it if you keep accepting unpaid work.

One aspect that can be quite aggravating is that you are not always guaranteed to get good pictures from a shoot, you may get no photos at all, or sometimes they might not be ones that are suitable to display in your portfolio. This is not so much of a frustrating issue at paid shoots, since you are still benefitting financially and the pictures can be seen as a bonus. However if you have had an unfulfilling unpaid test shoot and haven't received any notable pictures from it, you can feel like it has been a waste of your time, effort and travel money. If this is the case, try to see the positive side and think of it as good experience, a lesson learned and you will hopefully at least have made good contacts in the industry.

Tear Sheets
Once the model starts working, the aim is to get 'tear sheets'. These are editorial jobs that the model has done, where the pages have been directly 'torn' straight out of the magazine and into the portfolio. This shows that the model is working and the level of work that is being obtained. Having a tear sheet from the front cover of a noted magazine for example would be regarded very highly and would be a great asset to their portfolio.

In order to 'tear' a magazine page (sheet) out and put it in your book, it would need to be a 'full bleed' image. This just indicates that the image covers the whole page, as opposed to having a small picture in the corner of the page. If you were featured in a magazine and the image had an article written around it, the image of you would be small and therefore not one that you could use. Whereas if you actually had a full spread fashion shoot for the magazine, these would be ideal shots to have in your portfolio.

Runway photos
Some models that are involved in shows can have pictures taken whilst walking down the runway and these can often be put into the back of your portfolio to show the versatility of your work.

Other
You will also obtain photos not just from tests or editorial work, but other paid photo shoots such as hair work, photography workshops, look books, website shoots, catalogue shoots and so on. Some of these can also go into the back of your book as examples of other work you have done.

Organising your portfolio
The arrangement of a portfolio is extremely important, as the order has to compliment the photos, flow skillfully and all the photos should harmonise together.

Your agency will help you to organise your book and as you get more new images they will help decide which older ones could be replaced or moved around. However it is important that you feel comfortable with the order of your shots and the photos in your book, as you are the one that will be showing it to clients at castings.

If you do not have an agency and you are arranging the photos yourself, you should begin by removing all the pictures from the book and laying them out like a grid on a large, flat and clean surface area. By viewing all the photos together like this you are able to identify quickly which photos go together and begin to feel for the order of them. For example, you will most likely get 2 photos from the same shoot, which will be of a similar style or look, maybe one close up and one full length, these can obviously be grouped next to each other in the book as they would complement each other. If however, you had 2 obviously contrasting photos, from different shoots, with a completely different style and theme, they might clash next to each other and be so distracting that neither photo will get the attention it deserves. Once you are happy with the arrangement, only then put them back in your book. If you are unsure about any image, don't put it in. Only display pictures that show you at your best.

Everyone obviously has an individual portfolio, like a fingerprint, no two are identical. However they are all arranged in a similar way and generally follow these guidelines:

- The order of the photos should keep the clients engaged and make them want to look on through the book. If you have too many similar photos, they will just skim through or not even look at them all. A portfolio should display variety, in order to showcase your skills as a model.
- At the start of every portfolio there should be a clear beauty shot, showing a close up of the face. It should be an image that clearly represents you, although needs to be striking, as this is the first image that clients will see of you and they could judge the rest of your book by your first picture. If it is a good shot, they will be interested and want to look through you book.
- Try to alternate and have a good balance between close up face shots and full-length body shots.
- Try not to have more than 2 photos from the same shoot. The client would rather see variation and versatility between looks than lots of similar pictures.
- It is ok to have empty pages at the end of your portfolio. Do not feel that you have to fill up every page. It is better to have

10 or 15 amazing pictures in your portfolio, than 30 average ones just to fill up the space.

- Make sure you only put your best images in the portfolio.
- Start and end the book with you very best shots; these are the ones that will be remembered more.
- In the portfolio you normally need at least one clear 'body shot' normally taken in swimwear or lingerie, where the client can clearly see the models body type and shape.
- All photos should be vertical, to make the portfolio easier to flick through. If there were horizontal and vertical pictures it would mean constantly changing the way you view the book and clients do not want to be rotating it around to view your pictures.
- It is ok for some photos to be split across 2 pages and take up a double page spread in your portfolio. But you don't want too many of these, possibly a couple at the most.
- All pictures should ideally fill the whole page in the portfolio and try not to have any white boarders around the pictures.
- While most photographers use digital cameras, there are still the rare few that will take Polaroid pictures first to test the lighting. If you ask the photographer if you can keep a Polaroid snapshot these are often nice to put in the back page of your book.
- All images should be high resolution (a high picture quality to eliminate the square pixels that can occur when enlarging a small photo). No picture in your book should be blurred, unclear or less than perfect.
- Try to include both black and white and colour images.
- Make sure you always keep comp cards in the back of your portfolio.

Where to buy a portfolio?

The majority of model agencies have their own design of portfolio that they can supply to you, with their agency name or logo on the front and agency contact details on the back.

They normally charge a fee to get one of their portfolios, although it is not necessarily more expensive than if you were to buy your own.

By having an agency branded portfolio, clients can see instantly at castings what agency you are represented by.

However if you do not have an agency but are still looking to obtain a book, there are several websites, craft shops and stationary shops that you can buy them from.

Portfolio details

A models portfolio can be different to other creative professions. Artists, designers and photographers, for example, usually require larger portfolios than models.

Therefore you must make sure that your book is suitable for the modelling profession.

Details for a model portfolio

The standard size is usually 12 inches x 9 inches (slightly bigger than A4).

The clear pages inside will have a black paper insert, so that you can mount photos back to back on either side of the black insert and the photos will not distract from each other. You should not be able to see the other picture behind; black paper should cover the whole of the page.

On the inside cover (ideally at the back of the book) there should be a pocket or sleeve big enough to hold your comp cards. You should always keep comp cards in your book.

If you buy your own make it an attractive looking book. You can buy them in Leather bound, leather effect or plastic. It looks more professional if you have a nice book and the client will take more notice if you clearly look after your portfolio.

Enjoy!

Your book is an extension of yourself and it is something to feel proud of. Make sure you look after it, keep it looking presentable and feel great showing it to people!

Authors Experience

I once had a casting with a noted photographer, whose was involved with a prominent modelling TV show. Since he was so well known, took amazing photographs and had great contacts in the industry, I was very excited to meet him and make a good impression. I had been modelling for over 6 years at the time and felt that I had a good portfolio and was very proud to hand it over for him to have a look at. He took a scan through, quickly looking at all the pictures and then peering back up at me over the top of the book. I was expecting the usual sort of positive comment such as 'that's a nice shot', or 'good photos', but instead I was stunned to hear 'I don't like any of your photos, your photos do you no justice at all. I think you need to re-do your whole book!' For once I was a bit lost for words, I had obviously experienced criticism about the way I look before and had been in the industry long enough to develop a thick skin, however I had never had such criticism towards my work before. After so many years developing and improving my book, for someone to tell me to start again was a little devastating. I managed to get my composure and took his words on board. I asked if he would be able to take new photos of me, which he did and then worked with as many new photographers as I could in order to change my portfolio (even if it involved unpaid test shoots). Even though I felt hurt by his initial comment, I was determined to do well on the photo shoot with him and prove that I was a good model. This positive attitude paid off and I have gained some great shots and it also transpires that photographer was absolutely correct, since altering my book, my photos have gained even more interest and I ended up booking loads more work.

Composite cards

The next step after starting a portfolio is to make a composite 'comp' card, or also known as a 'Z' card. This is the models business card, showcasing an example of their work, which they can leave with clients at castings. The comp card should be approximately A5 size or 5x7 inches and have one clear (usually head shot) picture on the front, along with the models name. On the back of the card there should be 3 or 4 other photos showing their work. It is advisable to have both head and full-length shots on the card, including one body shot either in swimwear or lingerie. The photographs on the back of the card should ideally fill as much of the cards space as possible in order for the images to be seen more clearly.

The card will also include the model agency logo and contact details, or direct contact details for freelance models and the models measurements.

It is important to put your actual measurements, do not try to make yourself into something that you are not. It will not help you to get work if the client sees on your card that you are a size 6UK, asks you to try their new designer outfit on and discovers that you are actually a size 10UK and ripped the outfit trying to get it on; they will not be impressed. If you book work with the client, they will base the outfit they give you on the measurements stated on your comp card, so don't lie about them! It is important to be honest, as there could be a designer out there wanting to work with someone your exact size!

Your agency will help you decide which pictures to display on your card, however you will have to pay for them yourself. Usually they cost around £150 for 100 cards. Obtaining the comp cards can be expensive, especially when you become more established and choose to have more than 1 set of cards done. When the model is more experienced it is often a good idea to have different categories of cards, for example a beauty/ commercial card and a fashion/ editorial card. This is so clients can clearly see what sort of model you are and fit your look to what they want.

There would be little point in showing a client an edgy, high fashion comp card when they were really looking for a smiley commercial look. So it makes good sense to have different cards, exploiting your versatility and different looks.

Change your look

It is absolutely essential that your comp card reflects your current look. If you have comp cards made and then decide you want to completely alter your image with a new hair colour, cut, tattoos or piercings you render your cards useless and you will have to invest in getting new ones printed.

It is perfectly acceptable to change your look, many models have benefitted from a new look and actually gained more work afterwards, but you have to ensure your portfolio and comp cards are changed too.

Where to get them printed

If you are represented with a model agency, they will often arrange to have your cards made for you, they will pay for them in advance and you will be expected to repay the cost. Or in some cases they send you directly to the printers they work with, to collect and pay for them yourself.

If you are a freelance model, you will need to find your own print shop. Simply search on the internet for any recommended print shop as they should all be able to make them for you.

Author's top tip

If you are a new model, do not start off with getting too many cards printed, as the chances are you will gain new photos quickly through different test shoots and you might want to refresh your card with newer images as you get them.

Also, even if you are an agency represented model, it is still good to have half the cards printed with your agency contact details and some with your direct contact details. That way if your agency sends you to a casting, you can give a card with their details on, but if you ever need to give out your direct details, you will have one of those cards handy as well.

Organisation

This is something that some people are better at than others, but as a model, you need to be organised, prepared and ready for anything!

You may read this and think it seems like common sense and not something you have to read, but in order to stay organised, make sure you keep an accurate diary.

Update your diary as soon as you find out about a shoot, casting or meeting. You may find out about a casting, think 'it's ok, I don't need to write it down yet, I will remember when it is', but you may not and then you will miss it! There is nothing more frustrating or annoying than realising you have missed a casting because you were too lazy to get up and write it down.

Make sure you write down all the information needed for a shoot or casting, don't just make a note in your diary of the date and time, also include the location, who you are meeting and a contact number if you have it. A common error as a freelance model, is writing down a casting but not writing the other details and then not remembering where you saw the casting advertised in the first place, so you know you have to be somewhere, you just can't remember where it is.

Also, don't just rely on your agency to collate all the details of a casting or shoot for you, double check for yourself that you have everything you need. For example, when giving you the call sheet, they might have missed out one digit on the client contact phone number by mistake and if you did not thoroughly check all details beforehand, if for whatever reason you were running late and need to call the client, you would be unable to and could potentially lose the booking.

For a casting, or shoot, always bring what is asked of you. If they ask you to bring a black T-shirt and skinny jeans, make sure you have them with you. If you don't own any of the items, it is not a problem, but tell them in advance, so that they can make alternative arrangements, do not suddenly turn up on the day really unprepared.

Please don't think that this is mundane and just written down to fill a space in this book, organisation really is a fundamental aspect, as one that should always be reminded of (unless you really are super-incredible-deserve-a-medal-organised).

Model Bag

An important aspect about being organised is having a well prepared model bag. Many things in this industry can arise unexpectedly, such as last minute castings or shoots, so you should always have your bag packed and ready to go at short notice. It can feel like a lot that you have to carry, but it is better to be fully equipped than to turn up unprepared.

Items for Male and Female models:

- Portfolio
- Comp cards
- Pen and notebook
- Wallet/ purse with money
- ID/ passport (can be needed to get into some buildings for castings or needed for last minute trips away)
- Mobile phone (Even better if you have a smart phone- to check emails for last minute castings)

- List of castings (with complete location details, times and name of casting director)
- Diary/ organiser (unless you have one on your phone, to ensure you are attending castings in right order, or to add in any extra shoots/castings)
- Map of area (A-Z in London, Subway map in New York, etc)
- Body spray/ perfume/cologne (if you have been rushing around at castings you might want a quick spray before going in to see the client)
- Mints (better than gum, as you don't want to be chewing when in a casting, but you still need to have fresh breath!)
- Pack of tissues
- Umbrella (depending on weather forecast; it may seem like common sense, but as you can now buy small lightweight ones it's better to be safe than sorry. You don't want to go into your casting looking like you swam there!)
- Food (pack snacks, e.g. fruit, nuts, protein bars etc, as rushing around at castings can get very tiring and you don't always get chance to stop for food. So make sure you always have something on you as you do not want to be running low on energy.)
- Bottle of water
- USB memory stick. In case there is ever the need to transfer any of your photos to you quickly.

Extra for female models:
- High heels (stilettos at least 4 inches high, not wedges/ platforms)
- Makeup (mainly lip gloss or foundation for extra touch ups)
- Mirror
- Bikini (optional but useful- can be needed to see your body shape at some castings, especially show castings)

- Change of underwear (useful to carry a pair of flesh coloured underwear or strapless flesh coloured bra, if you end up trying on clothes at a casting)
- Hairbrush/ hair band (depending on your hair type you might want to brush your hair quickly before a casting and sometimes they will ask you to tie your hair back so have a band on you)
- Nail file/ clear or natural colour nail polish
- Tweezers

Punctuality

You can lose work if you're late, simple as that!

As a model you need to have excellent common sense and will therefore realise that you need to be on time; as it is neither good manners or very professional to be late.

Sometimes it can't be avoided to be late, if you left your house in plenty of time, but your train was delayed or the subway was closed, or if you had an accident for example. In these cases let whoever your meeting know that you're going to be late, or even cancel, in some emergency situations.

If, however, you are late for the simple reason you couldn't get out of bed on time because you partied too much, or didn't check the address the night before and then realised last minute that your casting was all the other way across town, then you are setting yourself up not only to lose the job, but also gain an unreliable reputation for yourself.

Modelling is your business, so you should put the same amount of effort into it, as if you were working in any other professional job.

Sometimes there are many places for you to travel to in one day, so to make sure you are prepared. Here is a simple check list to follow.

Day of castings:

- Plan your route in advance
- Know how many castings you have and how much time you need to get to each one (Google maps can help plan routes).

- If any castings are in similar areas, try and see them the same sort of time.
- If you have castings that clash in time, try to prioritise. You can't be in 2 places at once, so go to whichever castings you think you are most likely going to get, or whichever one pays most money. If you have time go to the other one, rush there afterwards, but sometimes you just have to miss things.
- Be wise with your time. If you have castings that run between certain time periods, from 11am- 3pm for example, don't suddenly go last minute at 3pm; give yourself enough time to get there and be seen.
- It is often advisable to turn up towards the beginning of a casting, rather than turn up towards the end of the allocated time, as they may decide early on which models they want to work with.
- Always carry a map of the area (or use the map on a smart phone)

If you have a booking:
- Plan your route in advance.
- Leave well in advance, allow extra time for transportation problems if needed.
- Have the phone number of the photographer on you (or someone else at the shoot) so if you are running late you can at least contact someone.
- If you want to squeeze in a couple of castings before a shoot, remember the shoot was booked, so that takes priority. If you are late for it due to castings, you run the risk of not getting the casting because you were rushing and then losing out future or even the current shoot because you were late for it.

Modelling can be stressful at times, so to make your life easier and alleviate any worries, make sure that you are always on time and always organised!

Author's experience

I learnt a hard lesson once with punctuality when I first started modelling. I had been booked for an editorial magazine shoot that I was really looking forward to. At the time I lived just outside London and had to get the train to commute in. I was familiar with the train times, as it was a regular journey of mine and I was not expecting any problems. However, my shoot was booked for a Sunday and I never thought to check the train times for any changes over the weekend. On arrival at the train station, I was told that there were disruptions on the line due to major work being carried out and there was a bus replacement (that I had just missed). After waiting for the next bus I was now running about half hour late. I had tried to phone the client to let them know, however unfortunately my agency had missed out one digit in their phone number, which again I hadn't checked! When phoning around other people, I managed to reach the client, who told me not to bother coming to the shoot, as half hour late would disrupt the whole day. I consequently arrived in London and turned straight back around again to go home. This not only cost me this shoot, but a regular job with the client and I ended up losing my own money on the travel fare. From now on I always double check all details, travel arrangements and phone numbers and that situation has never happened again!

5

Your body

Outline of the chapter:
- Having body confidence with focus on 'body shots'
- Learning how to pose (with emphasis on the different parts of the body)
- Practice exercises for posing
- How to walk a catwalk (with emphasis on different parts of the body)
- Practice exercises for catwalk

As a model you need to be fully aware of how your body works, looks and moves and carefully think about your posture and expressions. It may seem ridiculous to think that you don't already know all the details about your body, however when modelling, everything has to be exact and it is only by examining each aspect and observing yourself in the mirror that you can really understand what makes a good image.

Body confidence

A model needs to have body confidence. This means feeling comfortable with the way you look and not being self conscious or 'body shy' around others.

There will be times when you will have to get undressed in front of someone else. This is not to be confused with glamour modelling, as that is different and involves being deliberately exposed on camera. However, there are occasions where you do have to get semi naked, such as at a fashion show, where there can be such quick changes between outfits, you might have a dresser (someone to help you quickly get changed) backstage that will strip you down to your thong and throw the next outfit on you. Or during a beauty or commercial shoot that require you to be topless or nude, but be covered or posed in such a way that nothing explicit will be revealed in the pictures. Or during lingerie or swimwear shoots where you need to be comfortable with wearing tiny outfits.

Whilst it is acceptable to get changed in front of other models, or stylists, just be careful of some photographers that might get pictures of you while you are undressed. They may not do it deliberately, but there could be an occasion where photographers are taking pictures backstage at shows or shoots who could catch you unawares. So always be mindful of who is around you and watch out for yourself. Also if you are asked to change in a place that you find unacceptable and would degrade you, such as in public, outdoors, or in front of people that make you uncomfortable, then you are well within your right to ask for somewhere private to change and any good industry professional you are working with, will respect your rights for a bit of privacy whilst getting changed.

Body shots

Most portfolios require at least one 'body shot', which is simply the best or clearest image to display your body type. In the case of high fashion modelling it is usually full length and taken wearing a swim suit or lingerie. It is an image whereby you usually have little clothes on, however it is not an x-rated picture or glamour shot, they are tastefully done and are not revealing.

If you have any areas of your body that you do not feel at ease with, it is a natural reaction to try to cover them during shoots. However, if you are not 100% confident in front of the camera, your uncomfortable attitude will show through on the pictures. Although remember, there is never any need to worry or be self conscious about marks on your body, as your photos will always be re-touched and edited to make you look your best.

Therefore, if you are shy about revealing your body in any way, regardless if you are in front of the camera or not, this job will probably not be for you.

However, the most important thing to remember is not to do anything in front of camera that you are not comfortable with, some models do nude pictures, other's do not. Just remember photos last, so make sure you are happy with your shots.

Posing

If you are confident with the way you look and would feel comfortable in front of the camera, you now need to know how to pose.

From head to toe

As a model you need to be able to pose in an elegant, graceful and artistic manner in front of the camera that will give a beautiful shot. Like any other art form, working your body into different positions is something that you need to practice off camera, to give you more confidence in front of the camera. When you look in the mirror notice how small movements in your facial muscles or changes in your body posture alter your look.

It is easy to give good poses in front of a mirror as you can instantly tell what looks good and what doesn't. Repeating poses in front of the mirror will give you good muscle memory, so you can easily replicate these looks in front of the camera. The muscle memory you will get will make your poses seem more relaxed and more elegant (as you will no longer be thinking too much about what looks good, it will happen automatically).

Quite simply the more experience and practice you get, the more confident you will feel and the better your shots will be.

There are times when the photographer will capture your whole body or part of it, however regardless of where the shot is cropped you should be aiming to model from head to toe.

For example, if there is a close up beauty shot, but you slouch your body and put no effort in below the camera angle then this will show on your face with your expression. You should always model with all your effort and therefore always model with your whole body.

When posing the aim is to move very slightly at a time, it is all about slow controlled movements. If the photographer says to angle your chin down or turn your head to the side, do not move quickly or too much, as the photographer might miss the best angle. The reason it is best to practice first in front of the mirror, is that some of the movements may be so small that it may be hard to feel much difference between positions. Sometimes it may seem like you have hardly altered your position, but it could make a vast amount of difference on camera.

It is also important to breathe! With the strain of holding some poses for a long period of time, or holding uncomfortable positions, there can be the tendency to hold your breath and tense up. If you take deep breaths and relax it makes the shoot much easier.

Face

Your face is the most important part of the photo. There is no sense in having an amazing body pose if your face says something completely different to the rest of you.

When practicing in front of the mirror, try very small movements and changes with your eye, mouth and jaw muscles. Do not over exaggerate the expressions otherwise they will start to look comical instead of natural. Knowing exactly how your facial muscles look and move will especially help with close beauty shots.

Understand the concept and feel of the shoot, imagine different emotions in your head to match this and it will show on your face. Simply feeling the genuine emotion on the inside will subtly and beautifully show on the outside and give great photos.

Eyes

Your eyes are the main feature that expresses emotion to the camera and connects with the audience. You want to be able to 'smile with your eyes'. Think of things that make you happy and it will show through, think of a baby, your pet, your family or friends. Anything that makes you feel good and the emotion will be apparent in the shot. In contrast, if the photographer asks you for any other emotion (sad, angry, thoughtful) think of things that make you feel that way and again it will show through the eyes, not the whole face.

Always make sure you are well rested before a shoot, as if your eyes are tired, you will find it hard to focus the rest of your face. If you have been out the night before, drinking, partying or smoking, your eyes will show the strain and you will not get good photographs.

Sometimes your eyes can become tired when shooting for a long time, if there is bright sunlight, or if you have too much makeup on them, so there are a few tips to refresh your eyes when you are on shooting:

- Close them for a few seconds and ask the photographer to say 'open' just before he takes the shot (of course you do not want to over-use this technique. It can only be used best when you really have had a long shooting day, or if you are shooting outside and the sun really is blinding, you do not want to use it when you first arrive just because you got up too early and you want some extra shut-eye!)

- Look away from camera for some shots. Either look down and have a day-dream expression on your face, or look to the side and pretend you are staring off into the distance.
- Stare to a point directly behind the camera. So it looks like your looking into the lens, but in fact you are looking a tiny bit above (just passed the photographers head)

Neck

Your neck is a very important part of the photo. You always want to elongate your neck. If you lose your neck in the photo it can make the photo look strange and out of proportion. If you are blessed with having a naturally long neck then you do not have to worry so much in the pictures about this, as you will probably show it off anyway. But if you have a shorter neck, have poses that tilt your head back slightly. Or jut your head forward to stretch your neck. Imagine you have invisible string attached to your fore-head that is pulling your head and therefore stretching your neck out. Just remember not to lift your head up too high. Elongating your neck, does not mean lift your head up so the camera see's up your nostril.

Jaw

There can be a tendency to tense the jaw muscles, causing the mouth and overall facial expression to stiffen up. Simply by relaxing your jaw and letting your mouth drop open slightly, it gives a gentler, softer image in the face. However, small movements in your face and jaw can alter the photo completely. Try staring into a mirror, loosen all your facial muscles and then try tensing and relaxing your jaw very slightly. Take note of how the flexed muscles at the side of your face can alter your look and give it a slight edge (this can be useful for certain shoots with strong emotions or particular expressions, but do not over-use this technique).

Mouth

There are many different shapes that you can manipulate your mouth into. Just play around in the mirror with different looks. Mouth open, mouth closed, slightly parted showing teeth, slightly parted not showing teeth, smiling. Main rule of thumb is to make your mouth look natural, do not use the 'trout pout' expression by pursing your lips, this is only a stereotypical model image that no one actually uses! Just play around in front of the mirror and get to know which expression suits you best.

Hands

Be careful with the position of your hands in photographs. You want them, just like the rest of you to look natural and relaxed, however they can often look ungainly and unsightly in photographs and distract from the amazing pose or look you are giving. This is because your hands are close in size to your face and so can easily steal focus in a photograph. If you have your hands on your hips, try and keep fingers closer together. Or if you have your hands in front of your face, turn them so the thinner side of your hand is facing the camera, not the large palm or back of your hand. Or have fingers slightly bent, not straight so you look like sergeant in the army and not curled under, so it looks like you have no fingers, just relax them. Have a look in the mirror and try out different ways of using your hands around your face, so that when you are in front of the camera you will know what it looks like.

Body

As a general rule the more uncomfortable the position of the pose the better it will look. For example, arching the back, elongating the neck or wearing very high heels can all give a more attractive picture by giving a more interesting shape. Some positions may feel really exaggerated or bizarre, however they always look different on camera to how you imagine them looking.

You need to constantly be thinking about what would look good on camera, not what looks good for yourself. For example, if you just want to look sexy, gorgeous or good-looking in the picture, then you do not understand the nature of modelling. You do not get a choice about the theme of the shoot, so you should pose in ways that show off the clothes, give an interesting shape to the camera, look appealing and eye-catching and this does not necessarily mean looking good yourself. You could be wearing a bin bag with crazy hair and makeup, but you still have to make the look work.

Just like practicing different facial expressions in the mirror it is always a good idea to practice full body poses in the same way. It can be difficult to be aware of your whole body, but you should be thinking about every part of you; where you hands are, what position your feet are in, is this a good angle and so on. By practicing in front of a mirror before hand, it will make things easier when you come to a shoot.

For example when posing full length, standing facing the camera, if you bend one knee forward directly in front of you, it makes it seem like you have one leg shorter than the other. However if you turn that knee in or out then it makes it look much better like a high fashion pose and one that is versatile for many different shoots, or if you stand slightly side on to the camera it makes you look slimmer.

Try to alternate as well with different levels, not all photos have to be standing, they could be sitting, jumping, lying or kneeling. You just need to have the confidence to try different looks and if it doesn't work the photographer will tell you, but if you don't try them then you could miss out on a great shot.

When you first start modelling, find a few simple, natural poses that you are comfortable with and are fairly universal for whatever shoot you were doing; such as having one hand on hip. Then play around with that pose, but keep the same basic shape. Alter it so that you create 3 or 4 new looks, for example, altering the position of your head, moving your shoulders, altering the position of your feet or changing your facial expression.

Instead of thinking up loads of different poses in front of the camera, find simple poses, alter them very slightly to create a few more poses and you have several looks without trying too hard. It will also be easier for the photographer to capture the image if you are not bobbing around all over the place trying to get into different positions.

With more practice you will pick up techniques, however it is always useful when on a shoot if you ask the photographer to see a couple of the photos on the camera, as it gives you an idea on what poses work for the shoot and which ones don't.

Props

There can be the occasion where you have to work with a prop in the photograph, for example posing holding a cigarette, cup, sunglasses, football, handbag or whatever the object may be. You have to make it seem as normal as possible working with this item. For example if you are asked to hold a cigarette and you have never smoked in your life, you have to make it seem like you are comfortable holding it, know exactly what you are doing and still give a great shot. Working with props can be difficult as you want the shot to look natural, but don't want to over use the item or make the shot seem really forced, a prop should be an extension of your body and it should be used to enhance any photo not distract from it.

Examples of prop use:

Photo: Mike Hallenback   Photo: Stefanie Apple
Model: Sean O' Neill   Model: Rachel Woods

Confidence

A model always needs to have confidence in front of the camera, not just with their body in general, but to some extent with being a bit fearless in order to get the best shot. If the shoot is on location outdoors there is not only the crew you're working with watching you, but often the public that tend to stop for a look as well, so you cannot be embarrassed about posing. Sometimes models are asked to pose in a location that make might make them naturally uncomfortable, such as on a balcony or rooftop, or sneaking through a padlocked fence that says 'restricted access'. Of course you should not let anyone force you into a position or location you are really not comfortable with just to get a good shot. However, if you can have the confidence, it can be good to challenge yourself and push your comfort zone and who knows, you might just end up with your best photo!

Example of a shot where you need confidence:

Photo: Paul Colliton
Model: Elizabeth Zhong

Practice exercises

- When practicing different poses in front of the mirror, try to alter or move one small thing at a time and see how that one alteration affects the whole overall look.

- See how many different positions you can think of with keeping one body part the same. For example, how many different positions can you do whilst keeping both hands on your hips, or keeping one arm above your head, or keeping one knee bent?

- Decide on 5 poses that you feel comfortable with, suit your look and would be useful poses to have for any photoshoot and then practice moving fluidly and continuously between each one. Once you feel confident with those 5, move on to a different 5.

- Look through magazines to get some ideas on different poses and then work out the best position for you for; a standing shot, sitting shot and floor shot (3 poses, 3 different height levels)

Catwalk

Knowing how your body moves and looks whilst posing on a shoot, will give transferable skills for walking on the catwalk. As once again you need to be aware of all of your movements and have confidence.

Not all models are designed to be catwalk models for the major fashion weeks in London, Paris, New York and Milan. Getting to be one of the models that represent some of the big designers in these shows is definitely height and size dependent (meaning very tall and very slim). However, regardless of whether you are likely to be a run-way model or not, you should not discount the need to learn how to walk a runway, as there may be an occasion where it might arise.

Walking a runway can be a daunting task, everyone staring at you while you're trying not to fall over and embarrass yourself. The trick is to relax and enjoy yourself and whatever happens, carry on walking. Even if you lose some clothing, your outfit starts to fall down, your shoe comes off, you walk the wrong way or if you fall over, just keep going, act like nothing has happened and continue to strut your stuff. Whatever emotion you project, the audience will pick up on. If you feel nervous, embarrassed or shear terrified, the audience will notice that on your face and in your body language and they will feel so nervous for you, apart from the fact you will also tense up and find it more difficult to walk. However, if you look relaxed, at ease and comfortable on stage, the audience in turn will enjoy watching you and the show and even if you do make a mistake, no one will ever notice as you will be oozing confidence.

Your probably wondering how you look at ease in front of all those people, whilst wearing stilettos?

Firstly, come prepared; unless it is a big show and you have been for a previous fitting, you will usually have no idea what you will be wearing until you get there. So ensure you are well groomed and shaved, have the correct flesh coloured underwear on and a spare pair of neutral colour (black/ flesh/ white) high heels in your bag.

Secondly, whatever shoes or outfit you get, you have to deal with it, as it would appear unprofessional to make a fuss and demand another outfit. As a model you should be able to wear anything and make it look amazing (unless it is something you really can't wear, like squeezing your size 7 feet into a pair of size 4 shoes. However in this situation if they have no suitable alternative, you have your own heels in your bag).

Thirdly, if you're nervous you will start to shake or tremble and you will never be able to walk correctly, so do whatever technique it takes to calm you down. Imagine the audience in their underwear, take deep breaths, close your eyes before you go on and envision you are on a beach or count the number of people in the audience if you have to.

When you walk you want to use the outfit you are wearing. If you have pockets feel free to put your thumbs in the pockets and hang your hands off them, (don't stuff your whole hands in) or if you have a coat or jacket, you can undo it and swing it over your shoulder (however if you do need or want to remove your jacket on the catwalk always undo it from the bottom up, if possible, instead of top down like you normally would as this makes it quicker and easier to remove).

Finally do not look out for anyone in the audience, look straight ahead and do not take any notice of whoever is watching you. The only people you should be aware of are the photographers and they are usually at the end of the runway.

Remember everyone there has come to see you, they are willing you to do well, they don't secretly want you to fall over just so they can get some entertainment, half the audience would probably love to be in your place, so make the most of it!

Posture and how to walk

It can be helpful to watch runway shows on the TV to observe how other models walk, to get an idea of how to pose, how to turn, body posture and so on. However do not copy someone else's walk or style. What works for them might not necessarily work for you. To achieve anything in the modelling industry you have to be yourself, you will never get anywhere if you copy another model, as you will no longer be unique.

Step

Another main reason for not copying other models is that the other model you may want to copy may not actually have the best walk. There can be a tendency with some catwalk models to over exaggerate the step and it ends up looking a bit like a trotting horse.

Be wary of over stepping your walk or raising your leg too high for each step. The knee should come up slightly higher than normal and the step should be ideally half a step more than your normal stride, but still look natural. Step should be one foot directly in line in front of the other.

If you are walking the runway next to another model, pace your walk and step together, don't try to steal the show and walk ahead. Also don't always walk to the beat of the music; as the song can change quickly, or the beat might be too fast or slow for the pace of the runway show, so try to block out the beat and walk to your own pace. This can be difficult, but it will come with practice.

Arms/ shoulders/ back

The position of your shoulders and arms is equally important to your step. Shoulders should be pulled slightly back, yet still look relaxed. It can help if you lean your whole upper torso back very slightly, so you lead your walk from your pelvis level. Arms should again be loose and relaxed but not swing too much. They should swing less than in your normal walk down the street. They should also move from the elbow down, rather than move the whole arm.

Hands

If you do not have pockets and your hands are down, then make sure you do not tense up your fingers into fists. As it will not look as good when the photographers are taking photos, as it might look like you have no fingers. Keep hands open and fingers relatively close together. Just let your hand naturally flop where it wants to, don't tense up.

Head/ Eyes

Most important of all is your head, as the photographers will want to get a photo of you looking good. If your body looks amazing, but your head is not angled correctly, or face does not have the right expression, then it can ruin a perfectly good shot.

Your face should have a relaxed, natural and neutral expression with no frowns or no smiles (unless the designer specifies differently).

The position of your head should be angled down extremely slightly, just a tiny bit down from looking straight ahead normally. This is because the majority of photographers will be looking up at you. Your eyes should look straight ahead. Try to avoid looking down, as this can look like your eyes are closed in photos and it shows that you are not as confident. Look proud and stare straight ahead at a spot at the back of the room. Only look down if you feel you really have to, when you're going down steps, of if you feel you are going to fall off the end of the runway (look down with your eyes only, not with your whole head). You will usually have had a rehearsal on the runway before hand, to familiarise yourself, so you shouldn't have to look down at all.

End of runway pose

When you reach the end of the runway, make sure to pose. You should use your own judgment to decide how long to spend posing at the end of the runway. It should depend on how fast paced the runway show is, but you should give adequate time for the photographers to get a good picture. When you are posing, try to avoid putting both hands on your hips, otherwise you risk looking like a teapot. One hand can suffice on hip or loosely rested in pockets.

Practice Exercises

- Find a large enough room, ideally with a mirror that you can walk up and down in. If you can't find a good space to practice in, go outside and ask someone to video you walking, so you can see exactly for yourself what you look like.
- Face the mirror and practice turning (like you would at the end of the catwalk), for pageants/ competitions you turn by pivoting on one foot, however for catwalk you need to simply step back. Practice different ways until you find a turn that looks good and suits you.
- For women, practice walking in stiletto high heels, not wedges and ideally a pair of shoes that you have borrowed and are therefore not familiar with walking in (although ask before borrowing!).
- In order to practice walking one foot in front of the other in a completely straight line whilst still maintaining your balance, start off by over exaggerating the step and cross over your feet completely with each step. Find a line on the floor (follow the straight tile or wood floor pattern) and with each step cross your left leg to the right hand side of the line and vice versa, cross your right leg over to the left hand side of the line. Once you have managed to walk like this, tone it down and then you will find walking with each step directly straight in front of the

other on the floor line much easier (however remember that your toes also have to be facing directly ahead too, do not turn your feet inward or outwards).

6

Stay Healthy Stay Happy and looking good!

Overview on the chapter:
- General stresses and strains on the body that a model can suffer with
- Healthy diet and nutrition
- How to stay looking good
- What to wear/ how to dress

Irrespective of what type of modelling you are doing, the main essential thing is to be healthy and happy. When you feel good on the inside you look good on the outside. Most people think that modelling is all about looking constantly glamorous and wearing designer clothes, but it is much more than how you present yourself and about looking after all aspects of your body. This not only means taking care of your body physically by having clear skin, looked after hair, body weight and height in proportion, eating well, or keeping away from substances such as nicotine or caffeine. It also means looking after your body emotionally and dealing with the difficult psychological aspects that modelling can bring, such as coping with criticism and rejection. Remember you are the product that you work with for your job, so maintain your well-being inside and out.

Wear and Tear!

Everyone, model or not, suffers the daily stress of wear and tear on their appearance, such as dealing with the sun's UV rays on their skin, the cold winter snap that dries skin and frazzles hair, car pollution and smog. However, for a model it is not simply a case of overcoming these natural elements, they also have to combat against all the elements of the job. Standing up for hours under hot spotlights, wearing extra thick makeup that might also have been used by many others, hair damage caused by an excessive use of backcombing, hot straightening irons and curling tongs, wearing really uncomfortable high heel shoes and not only being exposed to the same weather as everyone else, but having to go out in it wearing completely the wrong thing, such as swimwear outside in the cold, or thick winter coats in the heat. Since models tend to suffer a little more than the average person when it comes to everyday wear and tear on the skin, hair and body, it is essential to continually look after yourself. In order to alleviate some of these effects try using face masks to restore your skin and deep conditioning treatment for your hair, avoid wearing makeup as much as possible and always moisturize.

Nutrition

There are many pre-conceived notions that you must be extremely skinny in order to be a good model, this notion encourages many models, new and experienced to want to lose weight. This desire to lose the pounds quickly can lead to eating disorders such as Anorexia or Bulimia. This is not a good lifestyle to have. Any job that compromises your health is not the right job for you. Do not let anyone entice you to lose weight; not your agent, photographers, or other models. If you start to drop weight too fast you can look malnourished and the photos will not be as good anyway. The best advice is to check with your doctor or nutritionist and maintain a healthy body weight and height ratio.

It also stands to reason that what goes in your body can show on the outside of your body. Try to eat healthy, nutritious food in the correct portion size for your body. Try to have your daily portions of 5 different fruit or vegetables. Watch your calorie intake and try to avoid fried or fatty foods, and if you are hungry do not deliberately starve yourself.

It is also advisable to keep alcohol intake to a minimum or ideally none at all (especially before a shoot), not to smoke or take drugs, all of which will age your skin prematurely and be potentially damaging to your career not to mention your overall health.

There can be a lot of peer pressure in the industry to smoke or drink, but you just need to remember that it is your career and yours alone that you need to think of. If you feel that the modelling lifestyle is too overwhelming, make sure you speak with someone; a parent, your agency or your friends. If your health is struggling, then maybe modelling is not the right career path for you.

Your look and body is your career, so you should look after it and treat it with respect.

How to dress

When you feel good on the inside it is also important to look good on the outside. The way you style yourself and dress can have an impact on your career.

Since modelling is a career where you are judged on your looks, you should always want to look your best. By ensuring that you are always dressed and styled appropriately, you will have the best chance of getting the casting, getting work, or getting an agency.

If you are still looking for an agency to represent you, you should still be dressing like a model, as this will give you a better chance of being scouted and it is good practice for finding out the best look that suits you.

It is a common misconception that you have to look glamorous, with lots of makeup or jewellery and designer clothes, when in reality simplicity is better. You have to find a balance between being too over-styled, with thick makeup and too much hairspray and being under-styled, wearing trainers or baggy jeans. Be your natural self and don't over-think your look.

Main fashion Do's and Don'ts:

Clients usually prefer to see your shape as best as possible, so either wear skinny jeans and tight tops or ideally (weather depending) show your legs by wearing a skirt, shorts or dress.

Try to avoid baggy clothes (no maxi dresses, long skirts, T-shirts or boyfriend cut jeans) wear close fitted clothes. Do not wear anything on your head; scarves, hats, head bands or sunglasses (if it is a sunny day and you need to wear sunglasses to a casting, make sure you take them off in advance to avoid making dents on your nose).

Bright colours are nice and can make you stand out from the rest of the competition. Although try to avoid any crazy patterns or designs and slogans or writing on tops.

Have little jewellery on, the client does not want to be distracted by huge earrings or a necklace and you don't want anything to take away the attention from your face.

How to look

It is not always about your clothes and what you wear, but also how you look in general.

Make sure you are always de-fuzzed. Have your eyebrows shaped and legs, under arms and bikini shaved or waxed. Since you never know when you are going to be called up for a casting or shoot, it can be really embarrassing if you go looking like a gorilla. So always be prepared and make sure you are always bikini ready. This also applies to male models. Skin should also be smooth, chest and back waxed if necessary, eyebrows do not have to be shaped as precisely as a female model, but any mono-brow should be separated.

No visible tan lines, do not assume that the photographer will air-brush your skin, as that takes a lot of extra time on their part afterwards. So if you really feel the need to tan your skin, make sure it looks natural and even and definitely no orange looking fake tan.

Make sure fingernails and toenails are looking good. Stick to natural nail colours. Either French manicure, or a plain colour like very light pink or beige. Try to avoid dark nail varnish colours like black or red, as these can often stain the natural colour of your nail. Male models should also have clean and trimmed nails.

Make sure skin is moisturised. If it has been cold weather and your lips are chapped, or have dry or peeling skin, make sure you carry body moisturiser and apply regularly.

Wear minimal makeup as possible or none at all. Foundation should match your skin tone in order for it to look invisible and all makeup should look natural; it should not look like you put makeup on in the first place. Makeup should just be meant as a tool to enhance your natural features, not completely cover over them.

An agency or a client at a casting will want to see what you look like, not what your makeup skills are like. They will see what you look like with makeup on from your portfolio and they will have professional makeup artists to work with you. So be yourself and don't cover over your beautiful face.

Hair should be clean and in a style that best suits your look and facial shape. If you are unsure what style would be most complementary to you, consult your hairstylist. If you have colour treated hair, ensure that it is well conditioned and regularly have the root colour maintained. The hair colour should also be one that is natural (unless you specifically want work as an alternative model). If you are fortunate enough to have an unusual, yet natural hair colour, such as a shade of red it can often go in your favour as a model, as it would make you stand out from the others. If you are encouraged to dye your hair for work, you should first consider whether it will distract or enhance from your overall look and consult with a stylist and your agency.

Depending on the casting and what personally suits you, it is usually a good idea to have your hair tied up in a ponytail so that the client can see your face and bone structure. However if the casting is for hair, then obviously leave it down.

Try not to mark your body with clearly visible tattoos or piercings (unless you are an alternative model), as they may be problematic when approaching agencies or clients. Unless the tattoo is small and easily hidden, they can often be difficult to disguise or cover when having a photo shoot. They could also limit the type of work you could get, as you would be unlikely to have any swimwear or lingerie shoot with obvious body art. Piercings have a similar affect to tattoos in the sense that they too can distract from your natural appearance. If you have one set of piercings in your ears or an easily concealed piercing, such as the tongue, these are considered acceptable. However it would be very difficult to get work if you have obvious piercings such as the lip, eyebrow or nose. Even if they were removed, you would still be left with a mark, so they are generally not advised.

If you have scars, birthmarks, moles, freckles or any other naturally occurring body mark, these are all features about your look that you are unable to change. Unlike the other aspects such as hair style, clothes or tattoos that are styled according to personal choice. However, these features can either be an advantage or disadvantage, for example minor scars and birthmarks can easily be covered and may in fact add a quirky quality to your look, although any major or obvious marks may unfortunately hinder or limit your career. Same as moles and freckles; a beauty spot or cheeky freckles could actually get you more work, as clients and agencies are always looking for models with unusual characteristics that make them stand out, however yet again, too many freckles or too large moles could limit a modelling career. Therefore do not dismiss anything about your look, if you think that you have an unusual feature that stops you from having a modelling career, you should perhaps re-think that, as it may be seen as an advantageous feature to have.

Above all you want your natural beauty to shine through, don't be anything that you are not. Everything about your appearance should enhance your natural look, not distract from it and most importantly if you feel good, you will look good!

7

Career

Outline of the chapter:
- Thinking of modelling as a career or full time occupation
- Working hours, income and the overall irregularity of the job
- Age: It's affect on a modelling career
- Combining a modelling career whilst still in education
- Chaperones
- Locations for modelling
- Travel
- The longevity of a modelling career
- Scams in the industry
- An overview of the advantages and disadvantages of having a modelling career

Modelling as a full time job

If you are really serious about becoming a model you have to think of it as a full time job. Looking for castings, attending castings and having photo shoots. You need to be committed, dedicated and steadfast about making modelling your career.

Do not expect modelling to be an easy career choice, it is a difficult profession to get into and even more difficult once you are in it. The 'average' model that makes modelling a full time profession really has to work hard to earn a living. It is the fortunate few that have an easier ride and break into the industry by being in the right place at the right time and having the right agency backing that end up becoming 'supermodels'. Do not compare yourself to famous models, or any other model for that matter, remain confident and focused on yourself. Each model has an individual career path, which is shaped and influenced by many factors and variables. You cannot evaluate or judge your career next to another model, since you don't know their background and you shouldn't let anything affect or distract you from your own journey. You may feel intimidated by more experienced models, but just remember that the modelling industry is so changeable that you don't know what will happen the next day, week or year and you may just find yourself having a more promising career path.

Working hours

Modelling is a career that is irregular and unpredictable. Your job could take you to any location, at any time, with any person, at very short notice. Castings and work can come up last minute and your daily schedule could change halfway through your day. It is troublesome planning things in your personal life as you never know if you have to cancel plans last minute to work, or there can be extremely long periods of time with no work or castings, then suddenly loads of things can come in at once. The working hours are definitely not 9 to 5. There are no set hours, a shoot could last anywhere from a couple of hours, a full day or spread over a few days. For anyone outside of modelling, they only see the finished result, the photo, so it can be hard to understand how time consuming a shoot can be. The irregularity of a modelling career is definitely one that can take time to adjust to.

Income

Whilst you need to think of modelling as a full time job, what you need to remember is that it is not regular pay and no agency can guarantee you work. Your agency can send you for castings, but unfortunately getting work involves a lot of different factors, such as how you present yourself, your photos, the way you are dressed, the clients opinion and luck. You may find that there are weeks when you are really busy, have booked lots of jobs. Or there might be periods when you have nothing, no castings or work. However, you might also find yourself really fortunate to have one really well paying job that will cover you for the next couple of months.

For the first few months starting a modelling career, don't be surprised to find that your bank account is slowly decreasing, as you spend money travelling around, money on comp cards, money for new clothes or on general items such as food (although remember you should be spending no money on getting photos). However if you put in the time and effort it should start to pay off. You will start to make more contacts and the more contacts you make the more work you will get. On the other hand you should not get yourself into any debt or financial hardship in order to start a modelling career. If you find that the work is not starting to come in after 8 months it is probably best to find another occupation, or speak with your agency if you have one.

Since finances often struggle initially with modelling, there is a lot of pressure to have another job whilst modelling. Although it is very difficult to work somewhere else, as you need to have the flexibility with your time in case any castings or work come up last minute.

If you have a night or evening job, it could make you tired for any shoots the next day and if you don't get enough sleep it will show. Or if you have another job in the daytime, there are very few jobs that are flexible enough to let you leave in the middle of the day with such short notice. As a model you need to be available for anything unexpected.

Age

Age is a fairly critical thing in the modelling industry. It is often widely conceived that once you reach mid 20's, it is too late for a modelling career. However in reality, you can be a model at any age; young or old. It just depends on the type of modelling.

With regards to high fashion modelling, they do have a preferred age range which for most agencies is somewhere in the region of 16-21 years old. This is probably where the notion of 'you have to be young to be a model' comes from. Since usually the first image that comes to mind of 'a model' is that of a young high fashion catwalk model.

There are of course some very well known supermodels that are now in their late 20's and 30's and still having a successful careers, however they established themselves when they were younger, made 'supermodel' status and have been able to carry on their careers.

Generally, once you get passed 25 it can be harder to find an agency, although not impossible. Keep in mind the age range is only 'preferred', meaning that if you are older, but are fortunate enough to look younger then of course you could still apply and still be considered. It is just a case of having more persistence and a bit more luck.

It also depends on what country you are modelling in. In the UK they prefer models younger, still in their teens, whereas in the US they are happier for a model to be a bit older in their 20's.

Nevertheless, there will always be a need for models of all ages, for catalogues, commercials and editorial work, as they have to employ the right age of model to suit the target consumer. If you feel you have the right look to be a model, then still apply to work regardless of age, as there are agencies to suit all different age ranges, it is just a matter of finding the right agency for you.

Modelling during education

It is widely known that models can start their career at a young age, around 13-14 years old. If a model is in their home country with the support of their parents, it does not seem shocking to begin a career at such an early age. However, there are many models in their early teens that have travelled to different countries to work, without a chaperone, left education and are living in shared agency model apartments without any supervision.

If you are under 18 years old and still in school it can be tricky to juggle both a modelling career and education. There are many models that leave school early to pursue a career and then have no qualifications to fall back on afterwards when they finish modelling and some models postpone their career until after they graduate from their current level of study, whether it is school, college or university. Of course it is a personal decision and it depends on the models situation. However modelling can be a fickle industry and there are no guarantees to the prosperity of a career and so it is often wise to have other options available that a good education and qualifications can provide.

Chaperones

Since many models do start their career when they are under the age of 18, they often have a chaperone when attending castings and shoots. This is completely acceptable and sometimes compulsory to have a parent or guardian accompany them. However, having a chaperone that is able to assist you with your career, whilst working around their own, can sometimes be problematic. Therefore when some young models have gained enough experience, they may chose to be alone, however this should be discussed with the chaperone, parent or guardian and the agency.

For adults over 18 years old, unless for safety reasons, it is generally unadvisable to have anyone accompany you as it can look unprofessional. A modelling career therefore can often be very lonely, as you will usually be by yourself, travelling around for castings and shoots.

Location

Where you live can play an important part in the success of your modelling career. If you are fortunate enough to already live in one of the major fashion capitals of the world such as New York, Paris, Milan or London you already have a major advantage. There is a wider choice of agencies available for you to apply to, it means you don't have to move anywhere else straight away and you are easily available for jobs or castings at short notice. If you live in a smaller town which is still close by to a major city with an easy commuting route then this too is also favorable. Since there might be smaller local agencies that you can join initially to gain some experience before moving to a big city and a larger agency. However, if you are in the countryside, where public transport is limited and there are no local agencies nearby then you are not going to get very far with your career. You need to be in a location where there is more work available, more agencies and more chance of being scouted. Large cities attract industry professionals and therefore this is where you need to be. If you choose to remain living outside a city and commute in, you need to make sure it is an easy journey, with frequently running public transport, as the last thing you want is to be at a shoot and worrying about how you are going to get home, or missing the last train or bus back.

Travel

As a model you should always be prepared to travel. This does not necessarily mean you need to have your toothbrush and pajama's packed in your handbag at all times. It simply means that you should have a valid passport in case your agency did want you to try a foreign market or if you had a shoot abroad on location.

There are two reasons for travelling abroad: for work (a specific job) or for the prospect of future work (more experience and to expand a models career).

The first option can be short term travel, usually booked for a specific job or shoot, the whole crew (photographer, MUA, stylist, client and model) would travel to the location. They would cover all expenses, accommodation, flight, usually food and then pay the models fee on top. Whilst this is an exciting opportunity and one that most models dream of, it usually consists of long shooting days, there is little or no chance for sight-seeing and it is considered as work and by no means a holiday.

The second reason is the most common, to further a models career and gain more experience. Nearly all models will at some point in their career try a new market abroad. This move will always be a benefit to the model by giving more practice and knowledge of the industry. However there is either the chance of booking loads of work and making a massive profit or getting no work and relying on your savings. There is no guarantee that moving abroad will gain you more work, but it will give you more experience.

Difficulties of travelling abroad

Travelling abroad can be difficult and exhausting for anyone; having to wait around in airports, heaving your luggage around, long flights, dealing with time differences or working out currency exchanges. Though for a model it is slightly harder, as you might work straight from leaving the airport without having a rest, you are expected to look good even whilst travelling long journeys, you might be away from family and friends for long periods of time, it is often very lonely and sometimes you might have to work and attend castings whilst facing a language barrier. Not to mention you might travel all the way and not actually get any work.

It can be scary to travel, especially if you have not done much travelling before and it can be even scarier going by yourself. Yet it can be worth doing in order to further your career. Staying in the one area can make you feel comfortable and safe, although it may not get you as much work. By trying a new market, you can refresh your portfolio, develop more contacts and get you more experience, not to mention boost your confidence personally as a model.

You don't always have to travel abroad, moving to a different area in your own country can be a good start, though if you are not even willing to travel at all then a career in modelling will be limited.

If your agency suggests a country for you to go to and you are not comfortable going, then be honest and maybe suggest a different country or area you would be more open to trying instead. You don't have to go somewhere just because they tell you to. There are some countries that may be better to travel to than others in order to further your career, as your particular 'look' may be favoured more in one country than in another. Different countries have different markets and you may find that you can get more work in one place than you can elsewhere. You will learn with experience which market best suits your look.

Finances abroad

It is always advisable to not travel anywhere unless you have the money to get back should you wish to.

Most agencies will offer you accommodation in their model apartment, pay for travel and possibly give you money towards the cost of living. However this is not for free, they will expect to be paid back and work over in other countries is not guaranteed.

So there is always a chance of travelling abroad with an agency, not earning much money and getting into debt with them. It is a great idea to travel, but it is best to be able to support yourself, find your own place to live and pay for your own travel. That way, any money you earn abroad is your own and you can ideally leave with a profit. The majority of model apartments are overpriced and shared with several girls, so it is usually better to find your own place anyway if you do decide to travel abroad.

Legalities

It is easy to work in your home country without an agency as a freelance model, however when it comes to working abroad in a foreign country you generally need agency support in that county to help you travel there and gain a legitimate work visa (should you require one). This does not mean that you cannot therefore gain freelance work once you have got over there, by all means if you can find yourself extra work whilst in a foreign country then that will only aid your career (although should you be sponsored by an agency, they can still be entitled to a percentage of your freelance earnings. Speak with your agency or read your contract with them if you are in doubt).

Should you require a work visa (depending on what country you are going to) you need to get sponsorship from an agency in that country (in order to find an agency in that country you can search for them on the internet and apply to them in the same way that you would in your native country, see chapter 2). For example, when moving from the UK to the US you need to obtain a work visa, usually a specialist O1 visa for 'Artists and Entertainers' and you would need a modelling agency in the US to vouch for you (as your sponsor), prove you are a model and help with the formal Visa paperwork. If however, you hold a European Union passport, you can travel anywhere in the EU for work without a Visa. It is best to check what paperwork and identification you need before travelling anywhere.

You are also still responsible for your own taxes even when in a foreign country, so contact the local tax office to find out more specific details. Always do your research as you do not want to travel somewhere and then find there is a problem legally getting work.

Safety

Your personal safety is the most important thing. Act in a foreign country, the same way you would act in your own. For example, if you would not go out alone in the dark in your own country, do not do it abroad. It is also important to be mindful of local customs or traditions, do your research before moving anywhere. Keep in touch with family and of course your agency and if you have any issues or problems ensure you speak to someone.

Linked careers to modelling

The longevity of a modelling career is often in question, as many see it as short term career which has no prospects after it has ended. Since many models start their career at a young age there is always the question of 'what are you going to do for the rest of your life, modelling isn't a long term option.' I however respectfully disagree, the longevity of a models career is a personal choice, unlike other jobs where you could get fired or made redundant, you are unlikely going to lose your job as a model. There may of course be times where you lose your agency or lose a job, but that does not necessarily mean that you lose modelling; you could keep modelling if you want to.

Should there be a time where you decide to leave modelling as a profession, there are many other avenues one can take:

- Modelling can open the door to the TV industry, either as a presenter or actor. This is a common route for models to take as they have already built up the contacts and know what it is like to be in front of the camera.
- There is the option of becoming a booker, working in an agency or with enough experience starting your own agency.
- Some might re-train as a make-up artist, stylist or photographer and use their knowledge of being in front of the camera to being behind it.
- There is the option of becoming a personal shopper, image consultant, stylist or nutritionist, generally any career that can give guidance to people about their body, appearance or health.
- Or generally the life skills gained through modelling, such as the increased confidence or the ability to meet new people and communicate well with them, are important traits to have and can be applied to any other profession you chose.

Scams

Industry scams are an aspect that models (particularly new models) need to watch out for.

As modelling is a career that people generally enter into for the coveted fame, fortune and glamour, it can be easy for some people to take advantage of new aspiring models by promising them all of the above. There are many scams that prey on models and instead of receiving the promised fame and fortune, it merely turns out to be an illusion and they find themselves out of pocket and down in confidence.

Main rule of thumb: Do not spend excess amounts of your own money. There should be no reason to part with your cash for photo shoots, modelling schools, or agencies. You might have to pay for small additional fees from the agency *after* you have been taken on, but not *before*.

Be aware of anyone that asks for money up front. If you pay someone in the industry, you should be getting good value for their service, however if they have already run off with your money then they have no need to assist you. The majority of top model and talent agencies are trustworthy, but still be aware of the many agencies that are not legitimate and only want to scam you out of money. No model agency will ask you for money upfront for representation. A reputable agency will only take a percentage out of your earnings, usually 20%, so if you don't make money, then they don't make money. The only costs that an agency could ask you to pay for, (after they have accepted you onto their books) are your composite cards, portfolio book, accommodation and transport costs if you travelling from abroad and are staying in their model apartment or possibly to feature you on their website. Agencies work on a commission basis, so it is in their best interest to find you work. There may be exceptions, but as a general rule no reputable photographer, talent agency or model agency will ask you for money immediately and there should be no reason to pay them for something they have not done yet. Do your research, ask around, obtain references, search the internet and find out before handing over any money if the person or agency you are going to be working with is recommended.

Scouts

It is very simple for someone to impersonate a model scout. They could make up an agency, false business card and say the right things. Since it is very flattering to have someone approach you and say you are perfect for being a model, it is easy to let your ambition cloud your judgment. If you get scouted, make sure you are sensible and confirm that the person that stopped you is legitimate. They many not necessarily work for an agency that you have heard of, but that does not mean you should dismiss them straight away. Do your homework, check out the contact details on their card, check if the agency is recognized, and check that the scout works for them. It is always best to go with your gut instinct. If you are with other people when you are scouted and the scout says that all of your companions could also be models, even if you think otherwise, then they are most likely false scouts. A real scout would not say to anyone they could model; they would be looking for something very specific.

Modelling schools

Modelling schools are generally not widely credited by agencies, as new models can pick up bad habits from them. Modelling is a career that can be learnt on the job, you will pick up more techniques, poses, looks and styles from the different people you work with. Generally modelling schools are expensive and there is no guaranteed work from them. There may be occasional classes you could take, such as walking lessons, although it would be unnecessary for you to spend you own time and money on modelling schools, as it wouldn't really offer much benefit to you.

Modelling sites

There are numerous websites devoted to the modelling industry, most of which are free or have a very minimal cost. So there is no need to spend a fortune on websites to advertise you, when most reputable sites are cheaper. Just surf the net or use word of mouth and ask around to find the best and cheapest modelling sites.

Photography studios

Some models may chose to go to a photography or make over studio to start building a portfolio. These can be costly and not needed, but should you decide to go ahead anyway and have your photos taken, be aware of how much money you are handing over. Some studios might say that you have to pay a large deposit to hold your shoot, usually around £100, which will be refunded to you at the end of the shoot. However the studio will then ask if you would like to purchase a couple of photos as they already have the £100 from you, it is a good way of them keeping your money and you end up with pictures that might not be that great.

Or some studios may say they will give you a free 'test shoot' but you have to pay for the photos or makeup artist, or some other irrelevant cost. You should not be expected to pay anything for a 'test'.

Guaranteed work

Another scam to look out for is any agency that can guarantee you work, as previously said, no model is guaranteed work, no matter how amazing they look. Getting a booking involves lots of factors such as how much the agency pushes you forward to clients, how many castings they get you, how you present yourself at castings, how much competition there is, whether you have the right 'look' the client is going for and just some luck- being in the right place at the right time. It does not matter how successful the agency is, they still cannot guarantee 100% that they can get you work.

Bragging about their agency

Any agency that advertises to attract new models but yet still brags about how successful they are and how they are one of the top agencies in the business should start ringing alarm bells for you.

No top agency advertises, as they have new models throwing themselves at them so frequently they have no need to go looking for new faces. They might send out scouts to look for new faces, or be involved in modelling competitions, but they certainly won't be advertising on the internet, or in magazines.

Protect yourself

The majority of people out there are not set out to scam you, you don't need to feel skeptical about everyone you meet, but if you generally follow these rules of thumb you will fine. If in doubt go with your gut instinct, if you feel something is not right with an agent, job or casting, then you are probably right. Trust yourself, don't let your eagerness to have a modelling career cloud your judgment, have some common sense and do your research and you will be on the right path to having a safe and hopefully successful modelling career.

Finances and being self employed

For many average working models, dealing with finances can be a stressful part of their career. Unsure when the next paycheck will be coming in, balancing payments with periods of financial drought and working as a self employed individual.

As a model regardless of whether you have an agency or not, you are essentially self-employed. Your agency will get you the booking and pay you for it (minus their fee), but you will be responsible for paying your own taxes.

There are different tax laws in each country or state, so you will need to check with your local tax office, since you are the only person responsible for your own finances and you need to make sure that you are keeping your taxes up to date.

It is therefore advisable to keep all your receipts, keep an up to date filing system and ideally a spreadsheet of all your income and outgoings. So when it comes to filing tax returns or claiming tax back you have an accurate record that you can easily refer back to.

Payment

Obviously modelling can be a lucrative career and like any job, you do expect to be paid, so what are the payment options? There are no set modelling rates for each job, it is up to your agent (or yourself if you are a freelance model) to negotiate the best deal. A model can either be paid by the hour or have a set day rate (if you are a freelance model, make sure you know your rates, sometimes a photographer will ask what your rates are and you need to be able to answer quickly without thinking too much about it. Your personal rates, if asked, should depend upon your level of experience and be realistic).

In general the rate of pay for a shoot depends upon:

- Usage: what are the photos used for? How long will the pictures be advertised for? Where will the photos be displayed?
- Exclusivity: Will the photos be exclusive to one company or location?
- The type of work: What is the specific job? Is it a photo shoot, trade-show modelling, commercial or editorial work, fitting or runway etc?
- The model: pay can depend on the level of model. Super-model, experienced or beginner?

If you are a freelance model, you have no agency to fall back on. So you have to ensure that you have all details arranged accurately yourself. Always check these details before you get to the shoot:

- The form of payment, (monetary, test for prints (TFP), Trade; clothes, cosmetics etc)
- How much? (exact monetary amount, how many edited photos, what value of trade etc)
- How long after the shoot will you have to wait for payment?

People can often forget or change what they say the amount is, so make sure you have something in writing (text, email or written) just in case.

Confirming all details before you arrive for a booking can save any problems occurring, as you have no agency to fall back on and chase up the client for you. Above all, place yourself in position of an agent and do not be afraid to ask questions such as 'how much does the job pay' or 'how long after the job can I expect payment'. If you don't ask, there is no one else to ask for you.

If you have an agency they can sometimes be slow at paying, (which is usually the main grievance for models) and it can be a struggle getting some agents to pay up. So always check the section in your contracts about payment. It can take anywhere from a month to several months to get paid, so always make sure you have your own record, of when you did a job and how much you should receive for it. Therefore when contacting your agency you have accurate information on how much you should be paid.

Again, always confirm with your agent how much you will be getting paid before you arrive at the shoot. If you are unhappy with the amount, you will have no basis to negotiate with if you are already there, or have already completed the shoot. Once you have done the job, your agent will wait to be paid by the client, before they will pay you. The agency will automatically remove their cut before paying you, however whether you make £100 or £10,000, the percentage they take will stay the same regardless of how much you earn.

Overview of the main advantages and disadvantages of a modelling career

Advantages:

Of course the advantages may seem rather obvious; such as the financial rewards that can be offered, the opportunity to travel around the world, meet lots of new people, the possibility of fame, have beautiful photographs taken with the chance to see yourself in magazines, billboards or adverts and have a career that most people would dream about and in all likelihood, envy.

Disadvantages:

All of this is possible, but not guaranteed. You might earn lots of money from one shoot, but then might not work for another couple of weeks, or have beautiful photos, but they may not be published and the chance that you could become famous is miniscule.

The main disadvantage is the criticism, which unfortunately a prominent part of a modelling career. Hearing criticism and negative comments, is something which no one likes to hear, although in this industry it is something that you will have to deal with. It can be difficult, but the trick is to let it wash over you and not take it to heart.

As a model you are being judged on your look, which is a very personal thing. In any other normal circumstance or any other career it might be considered highly offensive, however this is the nature of the job and what one client may like another may not.

If you get comments such as 'your back arches too much', 'your toes look like cocktail sausages', 'your eyebrows aren't even', 'your shoulders are too broad' and so on, you cannot take it personally. Whilst that can be hard to hear, just think that you are a model and people are going to critique you on how you look, as it is part of the job. Especially some designers that want models to be the exact size and shape to fit their garments and if you're not, they will probably blame you for being the wrong size rather than acknowledge it's their design that's the wrong fit. One thing to remember is that you should not have to apologise for any criticism about your look or portfolio. For example, if you get a comment saying that your hair style doesn't suit you, don't say sorry and that you will change it next time, you should be thinking 'that's my look, my choice, if you don't like it, I'm sure someone else will'.

Another main disadvantage is rejection, from clients at castings, agencies, or photographer's. It is likely that you will hear a 'no' much more often than you will hear a 'yes'. The modelling career is all subjective and why a model is chosen over another one is all down to the client's personal choice. It is frustrating that even if a model has faced rejection from a job, then criticism can be thrown in as well, just to add insult to injury.

What you can do however is ask if there is anything you can do to rectify the rejection. Sometimes you are simply not the look that the client is after, or sometimes there are things that can be altered. For example, I was once told that my ears stuck out too much, but I asked the photographer if there was anything I could do to rectify that in the photos. Their suggestion was to use a tiny amount of super glue to temporarily pin them back. It was easily removed with nail varnish remover and definitely not a trick to be repeated or recommended, but the moral is: don't put up a brick wall if you get criticism, try and find a way around it and keep persevering.

However, you should not be thinking that everyone you meet in the industry will criticise you, the majority of people that you will meet throughout your career will be extremely complimentary and friendly. You can make some good friends, especially with other models, as you share similar experiences and with photographers, makeup artists or stylists, as you all understand the industry. Remember it is always the minority of people in the industry that can sound very critical, however if you feel like you're not thick skinned enough then modelling is probably not the right profession for you.

Another negative aspect of modelling is that it can be lonely and exhausting both physically and mentally. It takes a lot of effort to travel around for work and castings, to be away from home, to pose for hours on end and to constantly make an effort to look good. There is also a huge amount of competition with other models, which can get very depressing. There can often be a hundred models turn up to one casting, for one place in a shoot, so learning to deal with the competition and rising above it, is an aspect that can take time to adjust to.

Also whilst it can be financially rewarding, remember there are times when you might earn no money, as it is a business where you are never guaranteed to have work.

Think Carefully

It may seem like the list of disadvantages is longer than the list of advantages, but in reality it is just a case of weighing the pros with the cons and deciding if modelling is the right path for you. Not everyone is able to be a model, it should be apparent by now that is it not just about the way you look but also about your character. Some people may feel that they have what it takes to be a model, even though they might not and some people may have exactly the right attributes, but don't believe they could model, so as difficult as it may seem you need to take an unbiased view of yourself and if you genuinely feel that you do have what it takes to be a model, the main thing is not to be discouraged or let anything stand in your way.

Advice from the Models

All models, both male and female, start their journey in the same way by building up their reputation, building their portfolios and building their career. Therefore as a new model, it is always useful to get the words of wisdom from the experienced models that are not 'famous' and classed as 'supermodels' but all have had successful and flourishing careers.

From the Guys:

Sean O'Neill (Photo: Mike Hallenback)

I remember on my first shoot I was excited and wanted to impress, hoping to become the next big thing! My advice would be; to be confident but not cocky, charming but not full of yourself and don't show any fear! Listen and take the advice of the photographer, ask them what they are looking for before the shoot starts, have a clear understanding concerning the outcome and the aim of the shoot and maybe the night before practice some poses. Most important be approachable and sociable, don't show signs of nervousness or shyness. Try not to speak over the photographer, although feel free to speak up about your thoughts of the way the shoot should go.

Troy Cannata

One thing: "be you." The industry is filled with all sorts of characters, the person you are will only add to the scene and that what makes art,

art. All these ideas put together to create a beautiful piece of work. I have been in the arts for 4 years, I love the people I meet and work with. It's a great life!

Teddy Sanchez (photo: Sylvia Bosolasco)

I've been modelling for over 5 years; love it and enjoy it! One piece of advice I could give to anyone new in the field is always be professional no matter the shoot; you never know who you're going to be working with. It also helps to always listen to your favourite playlist right before the first shutter close, that way you're in the 'zone' the whole shoot and you can channel the inner 'thunder'!

Volodymyr Kubatskyy (Photo: Rachel Thalia Fisher)

There is no specific thing you have to do at a shoot, just listen to what they want you to do and do your best (of course if they picked you, then they already think you are the best!). Every model has one look that they are particularly good at, (mine is three quarters cropped photo, when I am looking to a side) so it is good to learn what look most suits you.

All brands and clients have a different style. You can be one of the most famous models and then a simple unknown client won't even look at you because you are not the style the brand wants to represent. Just remember if you don't fit one brand, there is always going to be another one that you will be perfect for. In general, it's a fun thing to do, it's a cool experience!

Eric Stanton (Photo by Rakeem Cunningham)

I am with 4 agencies around the world. I first started with an agency open call and all I took with me were some digital photos my friend took of me in an alley way in Beverly Hills! These were just some simple pictures; profiles, close ups on face and full body in a crew neck T-shirt and some shorts. Then they told me at the open call that they liked me and would sign me the next day. So I did! My advice to guys who want to look into modelling as a career is to most importantly take care of yourself. Health is the upmost importance and secondly don't change. Maintain your Individuality so agencies and clients alike see something special, something different in you than the rest of the models.

One can become a great model just by knowing themselves very well. Photographers like to work with people who are comfortable in their own skin, posing isn't so important as much as living in the moment of the shoot is. As long as you are moving fluidly and with ease the photographer is more comfortable and guaranteed that you as a model will get the best pictures possible and have fun doing so. You have to be confident and simply rock the clothes or rock the lights and if you are nearly naked you have to rock the body you were given!

Kingsley Aerhi

Having been modelling for 7 years here are my top tips for an aspiring model: When posing for pictures, the main focus should always be the models facial expression, more than the actual pose itself. You need to compose yourself and be comfortable, if you don't feel at home it will affect the shoot. When going freelance, you can get work without an agency but that depends on your contacts, just put yourself in the shoes of an agent in a modelling agency.

If you want to be represented by an agency, go to open calls and go in with a confident and positive attitude; your demeanor goes a long way. Just think of it like going in for a job interview and if they say 'no' it is only because they already have some one that has your same look or they are looking for a specific type so move on to the next open call and don't lose hope.

Diet and health is also very important. Every model should learn to know their bodies, eat the right stuff and exercise, otherwise you won't get work and your agency will drop you. You always have to be in your A game.

Jake Choi (Photo: U-Shin Kim)

One time when I was shooting with a very established photographer, he gave me some advice on posing. The advice was to keep your body very fluid and flexible. Meaning, don't be stiff because it will show in the pictures and try to change your pose a little bit with every other shot. Nothing too drastic, just a small change, like moving the position of your head or your left foot, etc.

Bernhard Lieder

Practice in front of the mirror with your own camera, try different angels and poses in order to find out how you look best in pictures and just be natural; you are blessed by having a great physique that others have identified as presentable, so this should not be a pressure. Just act on a shoot as if you were hanging out with friends, but nevertheless, still professional! Try to build up chemistry with the photographer, which will facilitate the whole shooting atmosphere and result in great pictures! Networking is also very important; with photographers, fellow models and agencies.

Try to develop your own little 'model universe'. Although the best bit of advice: the modelling industry, is about 'watching' rather than talking. You can learn a lot from other models by watching how they pose, how they walk, etc. Make use of this 'open source'!

Sam Hathaway (Photo: Joanna Hathaway)
LOVE YOURSELF FOR WHO YOU ARE and WHAT YOU LOOK
LIKE, BEFORE YOU ENTER THE INDUSTRY. What this industry
is looking for isn't a particular walk or a particular way of squinting
your eyes and it's not necessarily looking for beauty, because the
fashion industry is swamped with it. What people are really looking for is confidence that can be conveyed in a photo or walk; and
that confidence cannot be faked. The camera can tell! That confidence can only come from accepting yourself and not worrying
about others opinions; which is very hard to do in this industry. If
you are rejected for jobs it is not because you are not beautiful, but
because your hair is the wrong color or your eyebrows are not the
right shape for the shoot. Just get over it. It's not in your control and
you will make yourself miserable trying to justify why they didn't pick
you. Don't take it personally and focus on the right things: convey-
ing confidence and being yourself.

From the girls

Cassie Higgins

For castings wear a simple fitted black tank top and skinny jeans, with hair natural or in a pony tail and little to no makeup. Never go to a runway casting in wedge heels or stilettos under three inches high.

Do not say negative things about other models or designers you worked with previously and never be late! Never lie about your measurements because for the day of the shoot or show the clothes picked out for you are based on your comp card measurements, so always update your comp card and portfolio.

Do not turn down modelling jobs that are unpaid tests when you're just starting out as a model. In the beginning it's about learning how to pose and work runways so any job even unpaid is good learning experience.

Never sign a contract you haven't read and understood clearly and do not sacrifice your values for modelling! If put in a situation your uncomfortable with speak up! And finally NETWORK NETWORK NETWORK! Meet as many people in the industry as possible and stay educated and up to date with the industry.

Lauren Henry

I am very new to the industry, but all I can say is to listen to the photographer and listen to yourself. Try not to take yourself too seriously or make yourself nervous because it will come through in the pictures. On shoots be yourself, be relaxed and the rest will come naturally! Try for every opportunity you can get. The more you try and put yourself out there, the greater the outcome and keep your head above any negativity, because if you let it get to you it'll bring you down and take the fun parts out of modelling.

Mathilde Dratwa

My first print job was when I was living in France 6 years ago and I have been modelling more each year since then. I would tell new models to always have their comp cards (and, if possible, their book) as well as a makeup kit and a hair band with them, because so much of the business involves last-minute casting.

Wear clothes and shoes that you are comfortable in for the casting, but that are also, obviously, flattering. Don't wear anything too close or high to the neck (it doesn't have to be revealing, but it high collars look odd on camera; like you have no neck) and not too many patterns.

Always act professional on a shoot. Don't flirt with photographers or crew and not even other models; it's not the time or place.

Bring a drink and a snack. Even though you will usually be offered food, it's always better to have a healthy option, something you like, just in case the options offered to you are no good.Good luck! Don't get discouraged if it takes you a while to get going in the business, it takes time and effort to get the right photos and meet the right people, but work begets work, the more you can do for your career, the more work will come your way. So be disciplined and diligent and have fun!

Madlin Raquel (Photo: Russell Dreyer)
I have been modelling for 4 years and the best advice that I could give to new models is to go into everything open minded and too not be shy or afraid. For new models it can all be a bit intimidating at first, but

the more work you get you realize yourself getting more comfortable and gaining more confidence to try new things or poses. You also can't let yourself get too beat down if you get bad criticism or comments. You get tough skin really fast and you can't let it bother you about what other people say.

As for posing, one great advice that I was told when I first started modelling was to exaggerate poses and don't be afraid to try weird crazy poses, that you might picture in your own mind looking unusual, but who knows, the photographer might end up really loving it. When on a shoot, knowing the concept of the shoot helps and feel free to ask if the photographer if they want specific poses because then you can do that, but then also try your own as the photographer might end up liking that too.

When it comes to what to wear...always wear heels of course! At castings always have heels with you and have no nail polish or clear-colored nails.

Marianly Tejada

My advice to aspiring new models is to be dedicated and to persevere. Sometimes, even if we have the talent it takes a little while to find that place that we're going to do best at. Be patient and don't give up! Rather than a beauty tip, the best tool you can use in this industry is your personality. There can be a lot or just a few models with a similar look, but the personality is what's going to make you stand out.

Stephanie Fedor

I have been modelling for about a year and a half. It's been amazing and I love every minute! I would say for any new models having confidence is major. In this industry people can be hard on you and it might bring you down but you have to keep your head up and know that if you want it bad enough you can achieve it. Second, when posing don't try too hard, just let it come naturally and be yourself! On a shoot don't act silly or crazy just be polite, yourself and professional. When going on castings wear little to no makeup and dress simple. They don't want to see you all dolled up and wear heels! Also, for any new aspiring models, don't step on people to get where and what you want. Lastly be thankful and appreciative for every opportunity you get and any opportunity you don't get don't beat yourself up about it. Everything happens for a reason.

Marina Baranova (Photo: Alena Soboleva)

For me, modelling is a great pleasure and really good fun. In my childhood I was always dreaming about being a model, although I thought that it would never happen to me. My parents and boyfriend were against modelling, so I left Russia and started my career in another country. All I can say now is that the most important thing is to believe in yourself, being completely sure that you can do it and of course the support of your friends and relatives really helps!

The advice which I can give is that you need to show emotion in all your photo shoots and give the right feeling that the photo needs. Try to think of yourself as a real doll, statue, monument etc (according to the nature of photo shoot). Don't take things too seriously, otherwise you will end up looking like your passport photo, (in Russia we don't smile in that picture) and try to have some fun!

8

Good Luck!

Overview on the chapter
- What makes a model
- Summary on the life of a model
- Summary on what modelling is really like

Modelling can be a once in a lifetime chance, so think is it not only as a career but as an adventure. You should seize every moment you have, every casting you get given and every bit of work you get offered.

There is often a lot of pressure to get the big jobs and publicity, people might ask "what jobs have you done?", "what magazines can I see you in?" or "have you done any work I would recognize?" and you always want something impressive to tell them. If you haven't worked for any names they recognize then you can feel like you have failed in your career. Just remember that modelling work is so diverse and there are so many different jobs, that as long as you have been paid as a model (regardless of the amount) then you have not failed. It should not matter what other people outside the industry think. Their view of the industry has been blinkered by the media and no matter what you say they are not likely going to understand what being a model is really like.

If you do not achieve the big campaigns or the high fashion run-way shows it does not mean that you haven't done well. To achieve anything in the modelling industry is something to be proud of as it should be apparent now that not everyone can be a model. It takes not only the right look, but being in the right place, at the right time and having the right personality and emotional attributes. There are so many factors that can contribute to the success of a modelling career that to have worked at any level in the industry is a great thing.

To determine the 'success' of a modelling career should be based on personal aspirations for the model, not by wealth or fame. Many people, especially outside the industry, might think that in order to have a good, successful career you need to have your name widely known in the media, be the face of several big campaigns, have travelled the world and made loads of money. However this is just the level of success the media has lead us to believe is acceptable, for many models success is when they have their first paid job, when they first see their image in a magazine, or even finding an agent to represent them.

Focus on yourself

The key thing is to enjoy what you are doing and focus on yourself, as it is very easy to start comparing your career to other models that you speak to. You might hear other models saying what amazing work they have done, how much money they have made, or you might think their portfolio looks better than yours, or they are slimmer or more attractive than you. This negativity will affect your career, you cannot think about what other models have done, as you do not know their circumstances. They could have more experience, been in the right place at the right time, they might have close contacts in the industry, have a look that is very 'current' at the time, or even exaggerating how well they have done.

At times such as general casting calls, it can be hard not to judge yourself against other models, especially as you look around the room at the vast amount of models going for one job and as the scene can look so intimidating to a new model it is easy for self doubt to creep in.

However, if you ever think; "I'm not getting much work", "why haven't I had a campaign" or "everyone seems to be doing better than me", the chances are you are not alone. What can be difficult to realize at first is that all models, unless they have had an instant lucky break, are in the same boat and all thinking the same. That they could be doing better. Just stay confident in yourself, know that you too are also a good model and have just as much chance as anyone else for getting work.

Modelling is not a race, it is a marathon. It takes time to build up contacts, establish yourself and start earning money. Sometimes it is a case of being patient and knowing that you will get your time eventually.

Am I a model?

The title of 'model' sometimes gets thrown around idly and due to this fact many people may not realize the difficulty of this profession. Some people may say 'I've done a bit of modelling' although what they really mean is that they have been to a photography make over studio, paid for the pictures and now think they are a model or may have done one small job, maybe as a favour to a friend or family member.

A person can legitimately consider oneself a professional model once they start to get paid for their work as a model.

Summary of the life of a model

Modelling is very misunderstood and the challenging nature of it can only really be appreciated by someone that has worked as a professional model. There are of course many demanding and stressful career choices, however many people do not think of modelling as being one of them, as the media and society have created an image of the glamorous and easy model lifestyle, however for the average model this couldn't be further from the truth.

It is not only a difficult career path because of the constant rejection, amount of competition and the frequent criticism, it is also difficult financially, not knowing when your next paycheck will be, having some of your money deducted not only for the usual taxes but also for your agency, or several agencies as the case may be.

The hours are unsociable and unpredictable and your daily schedule can change even as you are going along with your day. You may have last minute shoots or castings at any time and you have no set working hours. Although you can usually expect early starts and late finishes.

Modelling is tough physically, with having to pose in uncomfortable positions for long periods of time, dealing with aches, pain, cramps, coping with extreme weather wearing the wrong outfit choice, having your hair damaged with over styling, cuts or colour, skin suffering from excessive use of makeup and multiple product use and the exhaustion of rushing around to several different places a day.

Without forgetting the emotional difficulties of being away from home and family for long periods of time, facing jealously, balancing an education and a career, dealing with the pressure of staying in shape and worrying about when your next job will be. Modelling is both physically and emotionally draining and therefore requires a strong character to succeed.

Before entering modelling, really think about why you want to be a model and what you hope to achieve from it. If you want to become a model just to become rich and famous, you might end up being disappointed, however if you want to have a unique experience, meet lots of interesting people, have a varied and unpredictable career, have the opportunity to travel and be in front of the camera with your picture in magazines, then you are more likely to enjoy the profession and gain a lot more from it.

Unlike most professions, one cannot be taught to *be* a model, only *how* to model. Meaning, the natural ability or look must always be there, however the skills needed are only acquired through experience gained and learning on the job. In order to speed up the learning process, techniques, lessons, hints, tips and advice can all be given, such as those in this book, but it is then up to the individual whether they are able to transfer the skills they have learned into practice and turn modelling into a career. It should now be apparent that not everyone is able to be a model, as modelling is more than having the right look. It is also about having drive, determination, a strong character, energy, confidence, luck and good timing.

Hopefully you have found 'The Model's Guide' useful and insightful and are well on your way to a successful and bright career in the world of modelling.

Just remember to follow the dream, always stay safe, have fun and enjoy it!

Glossary of key terms

Advance: Payment given to the model in advance, before the agency has received payment from the client.

Agency: The company and office that manages and promotes the model's career.

Agent: Also referred to as a 'booker', an employee of the Agency and the individual that works with the model.

Audition: a meeting with clients in order to obtain a job, similar to a casting, although this is usually for commercial work which involves reading or learning a script.

Beauty Shot: Same as 'Head Shot'. A close up photography shot from the head and shoulders upwards, which focuses on the face, makeup and hair.

Book: A models book, also known as a portfolio

Booker: Same as 'Agent'.

Booking: When a model has been confirmed to work.

Booking out: When a model books time off with the agency, when they are not available to work.

Call Sheet: The written information given to the model informing them of all the job details.

Casting: A meeting with potential clients for work

Cattle Call: a general casting with a vast amount of models attending.

Catwalk: See 'Runway'

Checking in: Contacting the agency to find out the models schedule for next day.

Client: the individual or company responsible for the shoot that would book the model.

Commission: the percentage given to the agency from models earnings.

Composite 'Comp' Card: also see 'Z' card. The models business card, with a selection of their photos, contact details and measurements.

Contract: formal written agreement between the model and agency or client.

Day Rate: Models fee for a day's work

Dresser: The person that would change and dress a model, usually present for runway shows.

Editorial: Print work featured in magazines.

Fee: Money paid to the model for work

Fitting: Models trying on clothes before a shoot or runway show to check the sizing.

Freelance: A model working without an agency

Full length: A photograph taken showing the complete model, head to toe

General Casting: Similar to 'Cattle call', any models can show up unrequested.

Go- See: A casting which involves meeting a client for no job in particular. It is a meet and greet opportunity.

Head Booker: The main booker in charge at agency.

Head Shot: See 'Beauty Shot'.

High Fashion: showcasing the collection of top designers, or the type of model that would appear in runway shows or prestigious editorial shoots.

Model Release: written form or contract giving the photographer permission to use a models image.

Open Call: A specific time and date to walk into the agency to seek representation.

Polaroid: Instant snapshot taken of a model

Portfolio: See 'Book'

Re-call: when a model is specifically asked back for a second or third casting.

Request: When a model is specifically asked to attend a casting. Usually get booked in at a
designated time.

Rolling shoot: Ongoing set of poses, meaning moving fluidly and quickly between each one and not having to think too hard about moving between poses.

Runway: Raised platform or stage that the model will walk down for a fashion show.

Shoot: When a model has a booking with a photographer, where they are in front of the camera

Tear- Sheet: Pages from a magazine displaying the Models editorial work.

Test Shoot: An unpaid assignment, for the model to update their look or gain more experience.

'Z' card: See 'composite card'.

Printed in Great Britain
by Amazon